PRAISE FOR FACING THE CHALLENGES

"In *Facing the Challenges: How Principals can Survive and Thrive in Today's Schools*, John Fitzsimons harnesses his 50 years of experience as a teacher, assistant principal, principal, assistant superintendent, and school superintendent to provide practical strategies and timely insights to those who are serving as principals and those who aspire to those positions. The book is relevant and a pleasure to read."—Janet Bamford, education writer and editor

"A very practical approach to becoming a successful principal. Dr. Fitzsimons incorporates many of the tools (along with background information) necessary to be well respected as an educational leader. *Facing the Challenges* is a valuable read, as it evaluates all of a school's components necessary for a viable teaching and learning environment."—George Akst, former middle school principal and district science supervisor

"John Fitzsimons provides a very useful guide that can, if utilized by school principals, result in their self-improvement while creating a clear sense of just how crucial that position is to successful schools. It can also show superintendents and district-level administrators how they can constructively support and evaluate their principals. Equally, it can serve administrators throughout the district as a means to improve their performance as school leaders."—Darrell R. Lund, former superintendent of schools and teacher

"*Facing the Challenges: How Principals Can Survive and Thrive in Today's Schools* is an eminently usable book that practitioners can pick up at night and put some of the time-tested principles into practice the very next morning. The content derives from the author's decades of experience in educational leadership positions and is directed at the principal in today's environment. I wish I had had this volume when I was a practicing school principal."—Abby B. Bergman, former school administrator, director of science, and educational consultant

"Superintendents know and understand that a successful, forward moving district is only possible with an effective, thoughtful principal in every school. *Facing the Challenges: How Principals can Survive and Thrive in Today's Schools* is an excellent resource for principals, superintendents and all staff involved in school and district leadership. The author understands the issues facing today's school leaders and provides practical information and recommendations to ensure success in our schools."—Frances Rabinowitz, executive director of the Connecticut Association of Public School Superintendents

"As a practicing and experienced educator (35 years), *Facing the Challenges: How Principals Can Survive and Thrive in Today's Schools* resonated with me on myriad levels, specifically the chapter on social and emotional learning. John provides the SEL competencies and practices that are truly at the forefront as we support teachers in their quest to help our students. He provides entry points . . . to mindfulness and restorative practices that should become part of every school's culture. It is a must-read for both new and experienced and principals."—Melissa Krieger, elementary principal (pre-K–5)

"*Facing the Challenges: How Principals Can Survive and Thrive in Today's Schools* is one of most relevant books regarding the challenges and issues principals face today. I was particularly impressed with how best these contemporary issues can be addressed with practical resolutions and suggestions. As a former principal and superintendent, I find this book a must-read for principals."—Thomas W. Roberts, former superintendent of schools and high school principal

"*Facing the Challenges: How Principals Can Survive and Thrive in Today's Schools* is an empowering read for current, as well as aspiring, educational administrators. The author provides the reader with nontheoretical practical examples and ideas rooted in many years of experience on the front lines. I recommend this book as a resource to aid the school leader in creating and articulating a vision for their students, teachers, and community."—Pat Pinto, former director of guidance and department chairman for physical education and athletics

"*Facing the Challenges: How Principals Can Survive and Thrive in Today's Schools* reflects well on the author's experiences as a teacher and administrator. The strategies recommended have been tested in schools and proven effective. It's a practical guide for today's principal to use when problem solving and looking for effective strategies to deal with today's school challenges. As a superintendent, I would give a copy to each of my principals with a follow-up discussion."—Fred Stokley, former superintendent of schools, deputy commissioner of education, and high school principal

"John, I really enjoyed reading through your book. . . . You did a tremendous job on the topic. Reading through the book, I was brought back in time and reminisced of your leadership in Tenafly. I enjoyed it because I know you walk the talk! Bravo! I'm so proud to know you and have had the opportunity to experience your leadership and mentorship."—Dora Kontogiannis, former high school principal and assistant principal

"Dr. Fitzsimons is a lifelong educator with an amazing passion for his craft. In his book *Facing Challenges: How Principals Can Survive and Thrive in Today's Schools* he has provided insightful and straightforward advice. It is a must-read for a new principal. His attention to the importance of the social and emotional component for the modern student is spot-on."—Robert Ferullo, high school principal (7–12)

"The role of principal in a post-Parkland and high-stakes testing era is critical to establishing quality educational settings that yield success for all students. *Facing the Challenges* provides valuable and laser-like focus on sound instructional strategies and social emotional learning practices. It offers insights into how healthy superintendent—principal relationships can be nurtured in order to create productive and positive outcomes for the children served in our nation's schools. It is an important read for leadership teams who are serious about supporting caring, student-centered environments."—Lorna R. Lewis, superintendent of schools

"Years ago, when I was a school psychologist, I would have wished that this book had been available to the principals with whom I worked. It would have made it so much easier for me to convince them of the importance of including in the curriculum programs focused on the social and emotional development of the children in their schools."—Bert Diamet, former school psychologist

"The reader will find *Facing the Challenges: How Principals Can Survive and Thrive in Today's Schools* insightful, informative, and to the point. It is a refreshing alternative to the many tedious and arcane research writings on this subject."—Ronald Pedone, former educational researcher, U.S. Department of Education

"I am proud to endorse John Fitzsimons's book, *Facing the Challenges: How Principals Can Survive and Thrive in Today's Schools*. So much changed; the future belongs to our children, and we must move forward. Principals do indeed need to face these challenges. Bravo, Dr. Fitzsimons."—Alma Kalb, former elementary school teacher

"John Fitzsimons has been a long-standing, experienced, and passionate educational leader. He is interested in passing on his experiences to educators seeking positions of leadership. John recognizes the importance of having everyone in a system participate in self-evaluation. To this end, he created questionnaires that can be used by administrators to gain insights from their colleagues. John recognizes that data derived from these feedback evaluations can be the basis for productive discussions and system improvements. His book should be required reading for every student seeking the principalship."—Steve Rubin, former director of graduate studies in educational leadership, assistant superintendent for instruction, and elementary principal

"The principal's role is highly complex, stressful, and demanding. Dr. Fitzsimons's book, *Facing the Challenges: How Principals Can Survive and Thrive in Today's Schools*, helps new and veteran administrators cut through the noise and focus on the essential elements of leadership so necessary in today's world. In this book, principals will find tools and suggestions to focus their energy on what is truly important in the role. This is particularly valuable in this era when principals are called upon to do much more than simply educate students. Fitzsimons's voice of reason and practical experience gives readers tools and strategies they can implement immediately to affect positive change in their schools."—Jennifer Pye Gebbie, director, Center for Advanced Studies and the Arts (9–12)

"*Facing the Challenges* is a refreshing look at the basics of school leadership that all new and aspiring school leaders can learn from. In an age of constant reform and political interference in education, this book looks at leadership as a way to create a true learning culture outside the influences of our chaotic world. I encourage those interested in school leadership as well as current school leaders to read this book to reflect and refine their own practices."—Charles S. Dedrick, executive, New York State Council of School Superintendents

Facing the Challenges

How Principals Can Survive and Thrive in Today's Schools

John T. Fitzsimons

ROWMAN & LITTLEFIELD
Lanham • Boulder • New York • London

Published by Rowman & Littlefield
An imprint of The Rowman & Littlefield Publishing Group, Inc.
4501 Forbes Boulevard, Suite 200, Lanham, Maryland 20706
www.rowman.com

6 Tinworth Street, London SE11 5AL

Copyright © 2019 by John T. Fitzsimons

All rights reserved. No part of this book may be reproduced in any form or by any electronic or mechanical means, including information storage and retrieval systems, without written permission from the publisher, except by a reviewer who may quote passages in a review.

British Library Cataloguing in Publication Information Available

Library of Congress Cataloging-in-Publication Data

Names: Fitzsimons, John T., 1940– author.
Title: Facing the challenges : how principals can survive and thrive in today's schools / John Fitzsimons.
Description: Lanham, Maryland : Rowman & Littlefield 2019. | Includes bibliographical references. | Summary: "The book urges the principals, closest to teaching and learning to have the courage to take charge. It offers strategies and approaches that will not only enable them to survive but to thrive as well"— Provided by publisher.
Identifiers: LCCN 2019016330 (print) | LCCN 2019980847 (ebook) | ISBN 9781475846607 (cloth) | ISBN 9781475846614 (paperback) | ISBN 9781475846621 (ebook)
Subjects: LCSH: School principals—United States. | Educational leadership—United States. | School management and organization—United States. | School environment—United States.
Classification: LCC LB2831.92 .F58 2019 (print) | LCC LB2831.92 (ebook) | DDC 371.2/012—dc23
LC record available at https://lccn.loc.gov/2019016330
LC ebook record available at https://lccn.loc.gov/2019980847

After spending a fifty-year career in education, I had the privilege of serving with extraordinary educators. Many were principals. It is to those public school principals that I dedicate this book. They were outstanding men and women who cared deeply about the welfare of the children, the teachers, and the communities they served.

They are engaged in noble work, work that has a lasting effect on the social fabric of a community. Today, more than ever, they deserve to be valued and recognized by the communities they serve.

Contents

Preface ... xi
Acknowledgments ... xv
Introduction ... xvii

1 Voices from the Field: Superintendents, Principals, and Teachers ... 1
2 Surviving: Becoming an Effective and Resilient Leader ... 21
3 Collaborating: The Role of Central Office ... 33
4 Thriving: Crucial Tasks and Effective Practices ... 47
5 Building a Safe, Social, Emotional, and Academic School Environment ... 73

Principal's Questionnaire ... 87
Superintendent's Questionnaire ... 93
Teacher's Questionnaire ... 99
Principal's Survey ... 105
Classroom Climate Survey: Grades 4–12 ... 107
West Windsor/Plainsboro Regional School District, New Jersey, High School Bell Schedule ... 111
No Substitute Policy and Six Class Meetings per Day ... 113
About the Author ... 115

Preface

The purpose of this book is to provide a perspective on recent school reforms and the challenges facing today's school principals. Suggestions are provided to enable them to work collaboratively and transparently with their superintendents, teachers, and communities. Strategies and approaches are provided throughout the book to enable principals to improve their leadership skills and provide their students with a quality education.

The message is political in nature, for politics is a process of creating and recreating what is possible and best for society. The ideas presented here will require courageous leadership that is always enacted with dignity and respect for the work of teaching and learning.

In the mid-1980s, education, once on the political back burner, became high on the agenda of every local, state, and federal politician. Their interest was aroused by the report issued by the National Commission on Excellence in Education on April 26, 1983.

At that time, then-president Ronald Reagan, a conservative and supporter of states' rights, hoped that the commission would abolish the U.S. Department of Education, a cabinet-level department recently established by the previous Carter administration. Conservatives were interested in restoring school prayer and recommending vouchers. The report did none of those things, but it did generate the false narrative that the nation's public schools were in crisis.

Formed to study the conditions of U.S. public schools, the National Commission on Excellence in Education found that the United States was, as the title of the commission's 1983 report reflected, a nation at risk. The report was filled with alarming language, including the famous statement that, "If an unfriendly foreign power had attempted to impose on America the mediocre educational performance that exists today, we might well have viewed it as an act of war."

The rhetoric, to say the least, was overstated. The report blamed schools for the current economic recession and pointed to the loss of industries to Japan and Germany. The criticism of the schools continued even after the recession ended. Of course, the schools had nothing to do with the loss of industries or Americans' desire to buy fuel-efficient cars.

The commission's statement marked the beginning of decades of harsh criticism of public schools. Out of such criticism came calls for teacher accountability to be measured by standardized tests, and, in 2001, with the passage of No Child Left Behind (NCLB), the once-voluntary National Assessment of Educational Progress (NAEP) became a compulsory assessment required to be administered by the states every two years.

When Congress reauthorized the Elementary and Secondary Education Act in 2001, as NCLB, federal funding was tied to compliance with federal mandates, instead of need. To receive federal funding, states had to test students' basic skills from grades 3 through 8. President Barack Obama's Race to the Top enhanced the punishments attached to NCLB, which was not a law but a program. It was designed as a competition in which states that wanted a share of $5 billion had to accept additional mandates, including evaluating teachers and principals by the test scores of their students, adopting the Common Core Standards, increasing the number of privately managed charter schools, and closing schools with low tests scores.

By 2015, with bipartisan support, NCLB required schools to demonstrate adequate yearly progress (AYP). If they failed, they would be publicly labeled as "Schools in Need of Improvement." The overwhelming number of schools within that category were located in underfunded urban and rural districts, and served poor and disadvantaged children. These schools received significant federal resources.

School closures that effected poor and minority children were common and highly disruptive. Typically, the children were sent to schools that were no better than those that closed. The policy erred in assuming low standardized test scores were caused by "bad schools" that should be closed. However, social scientists have known for many years that low scores are highly correlated with poverty. In effect, the schools and their teachers were punished for their student's being poor. By 2015, with bipartisan support, NCLB was replaced with the Every Student Succeeds Act (ESSA), which continued the mandate of annual testing—a practice found in no other high-performing nation.

These reforms put the spotlight on public education, warts and all. They filled a vacuum at the state and local levels, where the leadership of the schools remained relatively passive in promoting real educational reforms. The states themselves placed little emphasis on research and development or on establishing statewide standards. Instead, they were focused primarily on enforcing rules and regulations, for example, the number of days in the school year. The states devoted little attention to measuring how much students learned in that year.

U.S. public schools have survived since the 1983 publication of *A Nation at Risk*, but they remain under continued attack. Their fate was particularly uncertain following the 2016 presidential election, as the Trump administration and its secretary of education, Betsy DeVos, were no friends of public education. Throughout my career as a public-school educator,[1] I witnessed many reforms, some positive and some troubling. My experience gave me a unique perspective on the problems facing school principals.

My message is simple: It is time for public schools to be reformed from within. Those in leadership positions closest to the classroom should spearhead reforms rather than follow the direction of local, state, and federal politicians, almost uniformly lacking the knowledge and hands-on experience to enact meaningful and positive educational reforms. Principals, as the school leaders, on the other hand, are far better qualified to affect change within their schools.

The vision offered in this book is not a one-size-fits-all solution, nor do I present it as such. Rather, I simply hope that it will encourage principals to assess their ongoing performance, identify opportunities for improvement, build productive working relationships with colleagues and the community, and ultimately create a safe and healthy environment in which students will flourish.

NOTE

1. I served for 50 years in public education, 28 years as a school superintendent, 4 years as an assistant superintendent for curriculum and instruction, 3 as an elementary and assistant middle school principal, and 15 as a language arts coordinator and elementary school teacher.

Acknowledgments

This book would not have been possible without the generous and thoughtful responses I received from colleagues and educators both practicing and retired. Special thanks go to the cooperation I received from Lew Smith, executive director of the National Principals Institute (NPLI). They graciously agreed to have their participants at their 21st annual institute respond to the principal's survey following a review of the principal's questionnaire. The responses were essential in capturing the voices of principals from throughout the country.

In addition, I would like to thank Dr. Vicky Karant, Dr. Fred Stokley, Mr. Thomas Roberts, and Dr. Darrell Lund, fellow superintendents and colleagues with more than 100 years of experience serving public schools. Their insights and recommendations helped me to shape the manuscript into a practical and realistic guide that would well serve todays principals.

Several school principals who I have worked with throughout the years were quick to respond as readers of the manuscript and provided me with valuable recommendations based on their years of experience administering schools. They include Dr. Abby Bergman, Mr. George Akst, Dr. Dora Kontogiannis, Ms. Mellisa Krieger, Dr. Maureen Fitzpatrick, Mr. Robert Ferullo, and Dr. Steve Rubin. A special thanks to Mr. Dennis J. Lepold, high school principal, for sharing the school's six-period rotating schedule and their no-substitute policy.

I was fortunate to have friends that have served as school counselors, psychologists, educational researchers at the U.S. Department of Education, classroom teachers, and athletic coaches, all of whom deserve thanks for their timely and helpful suggestions, including the preface and introduction, as well as each chapter. They include Mr. Pat Pinto, counselor and athletic director; Dr. Bert Diament, school psychologist; Mr. Ronald Pedone, educational researcher; and Mr. Dennis Kavanagh, high school English teacher and Peace Core volunteer.

I would be remiss if I did not acknowledge Alma Kalb, my 92-year-old neighbor, who graduated from City University of New York and Columbia's Teachers College. She taught at the elementary level for 45 years and is still as sharp as any 29-year-old. She cheered me on throughout the writing process and spoke of the importance of a child-centered classroom and how she was greatly influenced by the teachings of John Dewey, a giant at Teachers College.

In addition, I owe a big thank you to my other wonderful neighbor and friend, Professor Charles Mayer, who was kind enough to read the entire manuscript with the discerning eye of an experienced teacher and scholar. His keen insights and suggestions truly enhanced the quality of my writing.

Lastly, and most deserving, I owe a special thanks to my wife, Dr. Carol Fitzsimons, for her support and encouragement throughout the writing of the book.

Introduction

This book begins with an attempt to capture the crucial voices in the field, which include principals, teachers, and superintendents. It begins with a challenge to school principals to assess their performance through a detailed questionnaire and share their responses with their superintendents and teachers.

The goal in the first chapter is to use the evaluations found in each questionnaire to begin a constructive conversation between the principal and the superintendent, as well as between the principal and the teachers. The intent is to flatten the hierarchy to establish more open, transparent, and trusting relationships among the educators in this period of disruptive and questionable educational reforms.

Thus, the book begins with a challenge to principals to share their self-evaluations of their performance as detailed in the principal's questionnaire. The exercise requires courage, for that is an essential attribute of effective leadership. The process will result in a healthier social, emotional, and collaborative school culture. Principals attending a weeklong symposium held by the National Principals Leadership Institute in New York City completed a survey (see appendix D) on the use of the questionnaires, as did a selection of principals not in attendance. Their responses are detailed in chapter 1.

The second chapter, entitled "Surviving: Becoming an Effective and Resilient Leader," is a natural follow-up to the first chapter, and the issues it discusses are timely ones. To survive, principals need to understand school governance issues. Thus, the chapter provides a model that identifies the number and positions of the various governing bodies that influence and control the public schools. Tied closely to the governance of the schools are the funding inequities created by the current practice of local control that plagues school districts throughout the country. What is cited in this chapter must be understood and appreciated by school principals if they are to survive and understand the parameters operating in today's schools.

Chapter 2 follows up with arguments for the support of teacher unions and points out that union leaders in many parts of the country have done little to improve the rank and file's depressed salaries and benefits. As a result, the chapter highlights the wildcat teacher strikes throughout the country, the national attention they have received, and the role such strikes have played in motivating many teachers to run for political office.

The third chapter moves beyond the confines of the school and highlights the importance of maintaining a close working relationship with the central office administrators and especially with the superintendent. The message is simple: No system can survive and thrive if the crucial actors remain isolated in their silos.

The fourth chapter, in keeping with the other themes of the book, outlines the key tasks that must be mastered to thrive as a school principal. Principals must not only master routine tasks, but also be challenged to examine current administrative practices, identify the political and educational impediments encountered, and test possible solutions.

The fifth and final chapter stresses the necessity of developing a safe and healthy social and emotional learning environment that includes the practices of restorative justice, mindfulness, and meditation, supported by years of research—something that is missing from many current school reforms. The suggestions noted throughout this book are presented in the spirit of helping today's principals navigate through difficult and challenging times and issues.

When enlightened school principals do everything they can to ensure that children are educated in a kind, caring, and compassionate school setting, our society will be populated with lifelong learners who are engaged citizens capable of making their lives and the lives of those in their communities safe, secure, and fruitful.

ONE
Voices from the Field

Superintendents, Principals, and Teachers

> We do not learn from experience . . . we learn from reflecting on experience. —John Dewey

The primary purpose of this book is to enable principals to build a healthy, social, emotional, and collaborative school culture amid the troubling number of educational reforms. For that to happen, principals must begin by examining and evaluating their work as principals. Being asked to stop and listen to the voices nearest to them as a means of improving their performance may not be what principals want to hear. Nevertheless, when faced with growing challenges, why not seek support from those who occupy the same space? Now, more than ever, is a time to ensure that schools are safe and secure while remaining quality educational institutions.

Today's school principals are faced with many challenges, be they in rural, suburban, or urban communities. Principals are held accountable for the day-to-day administration of the school system, and expectations are high from everyone they serve. Knowing how many challenges principals face in today's schools—including the ever-present challenge of keeping pace with technology, the politics of education, and the horrific reality of school shootings—asking principals to take the time to examine their performance may be more than they can reasonably tolerate.

CREATING A LEARNING CULTURE

A true community of learners is not likely to emerge without the leadership of the principal. For principals to survive and thrive in today's schools, they must reflect on and evaluate their overall effectiveness with help from those they interact with daily. Principals will be required to exercise confidence, self-assurance, and courageous leadership imbued with the elements and attributes found in servant, moral, and transformative leaders.

If principals remain isolated in their silos and lean too much on their positional power and control, the likelihood of improving learning conditions will remain slim. If their voices remain a mere whisper in the shadows of a culture that remains fearful of failure, suspicious of intentions and distrustful, no one in the system will grow and improve. Improving the effectiveness of one's performance can best begin by hearing and capturing the voices nearest to oneself.

THE QUESTIONNAIRES

To create a true learning culture and facilitate the essential first steps, the author constructed three questionnaires (see appendixes A, B, and C). The purpose of the questionnaires is to "kick-start" essential and crucial conversations, and they are to be used by the superintendent, teachers, and principal in their districts.

Although a four-point performance-rating scale is included in each questionnaire, the principal must be clear that they are not to be used as part of a formal evaluation. It is paramount that the principal spend the time necessary to assure teachers that the questionnaires are for the school's use only. They are designed as tools to provoke conversations about missions, goals, and how those responsible can effectively meet them.

Likewise, the questionnaires are not intended to support or test any educational theory or to be used as part of a research project. They are simply to be used as a means of gaining perceptions and opinions from every educator in the school organization. The analysis or interpretation of the responses to the questionnaires is left to the participants, who must weigh, evaluate, and act on their findings.

It will not be easy. The first step is for a principal to ask for a sit-down, face-to-face meeting with their superintendent and beginning the conversation with a simple request: "I think it best that we take some time to stop and reflect on our level of effectiveness, just as we require of our teachers. Why not examine how we are working together toward meeting the district's mission and goals?" Most superintendents would be highly receptive to that idea, if framed as a call to work openly and collaboratively.

The next step is for the principal to sit down face-to-face with their teacher leaders, most likely their building union representative, and make the same request. Here, too, the response is sure to be positive if the request is conveyed as a genuine call to build a strong team of colleagues to best serve the children in their care.

Principals may not be so sure that this approach will work in their district. They may be in a district that sees itself as a quality school system. They may be quick to point to their graduates who were accepted to Ivy League schools and their almost 100 percent graduation rate. They may view themselves as great educational leaders and see no need for time-consuming collaboration. *We ain't broke, so don't try to fix us* is the dominant attitude.

Principals who find themselves in such a situation can choose to sit by and practice what is called laissez-faire leadership, but that is neither a good situation to be faced with nor an option that most courageous leaders would take. Most likely, the school has become complacent and a bit arrogant, and in need of improvement—a common condition found in many wealthy suburban districts.

On the other hand, those principals in impoverished and under-resourced school districts where there are high levels of anxiety and fear of failure, and where educators are confronted with a challenging population, large class sizes, and frequent turnover of administrators and teachers, are sure to face many challenges, as well as resistance. Teachers may be exhausted and demoralized from responding to one crisis after another, with no end in sight. With the absence of strong leadership, rather than coming together, people will hunker down to cope and survive in whatever area of freedom and autonomy they control.

Principals in such a system are far more likely to see the school as broken and act as strong, insightful, and transformational leaders. Regardless of where one finds oneself, there is always a need for courageous leadership. Every district has its unique challenges. Principals who find themselves in a school where the climate is just short of toxic have a lot of work ahead of them. It will not be easy, and there are sure to be setbacks. Changing a school's culture takes a great deal of effort on everyone's part, but that process begins with the principal.

It is important for principals to remember why people are drawn to the teaching profession. Teaching naturally provides for a good degree of autonomy. Teachers like the idea that they can close their door and teach with little oversight from supervisors. In general, it is a condition that every professional desires. No matter the overall teaching conditions in a school, teachers seek and enjoy a degree of autonomy.

Principals must respect and be sensitive to that boundary by conveying a genuine need for collegiality and collaboration. They must lower and diminish their positional power by being more visible and approachable, and, by all means, be good listeners. There will always be some tension between the desire to be left alone to teach and the needs of the school system. Principals must learn to navigate these waters.

Those who seek out the principalship know there will be hills to climb. Leadership positions attract people who like challenges and are not intimated when faced with problems but work to solve them once they arrive at the foot of the hill; however, they may find themselves in muck. There is no surefire recipe to becoming an effective principal. Nonetheless, a key attribute of leadership is self-reliance. It is time to lead, and the first place to look for help is within. Thus, principals must take the time to mine their inner strengths and values.

Principals need to be open to input from those around them while remaining focused and energized, as well as maintaining a clear vision of where they want to go. To survive and thrive in today's schools, they must continuously reflect on and evaluate their overall effectiveness with help from those they serve. Improving the effectiveness of their performance can best begin by hearing and capturing the voices closest to them.

THREE QUESTIONNAIRES

The first questionnaire is designed for the district superintendent. It includes a self-evaluation of the superintendent's job performance. Once completed, it is best shared with the principal. The intent is to flatten the traditional hierarchy and create the opportunity for an open and honest discussion to take place between the principal and the superintendent. It is idealistic and would require a level of trust between the superintendent and the principal that may or may not exist. Nevertheless, it is worth trying even if initially rejected by the superintendent.

The second questionnaire is designed to capture principals' perceptions and opinions of their own work. It includes a rating scale of their job performance. When completed, it is to be shared with the superintendent and teachers. Here, too, the intent is to create the opportunity for an open and honest discussion to take place between the principal and the superintendent, and, in turn, between the principal and teachers.

It will require the principal to be secure and confident in their leadership ability, and, above all, be honest with their self-evaluation. They will inevitably receive harsh criticism that can sting and hurt if they take it personally. Rather, they must consider the source and the need to shrink one's ego throughout the process.

The third questionnaire is designed to access the opinions and perceptions of the teachers. It includes a rating scale of the principal's job performance. Once completed, it is shared with the principal. Principals need to demonstrate openness and a genuine desire to improve their performance to better serve teachers and students. The result will be the development of a learning community built on trust and collaboration. Asking those who one supervises to evaluate one's performance will not be easy, especially if the school lacks a high level of collegiality and is a school culture in which teachers work in isolation and rarely speak openly about their work.

THE SUPERINTENDENT'S VOICE

The superintendent's questionnaire (see appendix B) will provide principals with an understanding of how the superintendent judges his or her own job performance using the 1 to 4 ranking scale. It is the same scale most often used when evaluating teachers. The scale consists of the following ranks: 1) ineffective, 2) developing, 3) effective, and 4) highly effective. The superintendent's job performance is based on a list of tasks found in the literature as being in the scope and responsibility of the position.[1] It begins with "Defining the District's Mission" and ends with "Maintaining Clean and Attractive Buildings and Grounds." In addition, superintendents are asked to judge their time spent on six major functions, their use of power, and their leadership style.

The superintendent's questionnaire includes information on what the superintendent perceived as challenges, how he or she overcame them, and who prepared them for the position and how. The responses to such questions enable principals to determine if they coincide with the views of the superintendent's self-assessment and their working experiences with the superintendent. The intent of the questionnaire is to establish as much transparency as possible between the principal and superintendent, and induce a more collaborative professional relationship.

THE PRINCIPAL'S VOICE

The principal's questionnaire (see appendix A) asks the principal to rank his or her job performance using the same 1 to 4 rating scale. Principals are asked to rank their job performance on tasks generally agreed on in the literature as being in the scope and responsibility of the position.[2] The list begins with "Defining the School Mission" and ends with "Providing a Clean and Attractive School and Grounds." As with the superintendent's questionnaire, there are a number of questions regarding the challenges principals face, how they overcame them, and how they distribute their time among four major functions. In addition, there are several questions regarding the use of power and style of leadership.

Once a principal has completed the questionnaire, it is distributed to the superintendent and the teachers. The principal's response to the questionnaire will enable teachers to not only gain insights as to how their principal evaluated his or her own performance and work functions, but also, more importantly, see if the principal's answers coincide with the views of the teachers and the teachers' work experiences with him or her. Divergence can provide fertile grounds in which to gain clarification or for developing improvement plans, whereas, when convergence occurs, these are the areas that need to be nurtured and sustained. Again, the idea is to establish as much openness as possible between the principal and teachers with the goal of building highly collaborative working relationships.

THE TEACHERS' VOICES

Teachers are asked on their questionnaire (see appendix C) to rank the principal's job performance using the 1 to 4 rating scale, with the additional option of DK, don't know. Here, too, the intent is to create the opportunity for an open and honest discussion between the principal and teachers. The purpose is to improve working conditions in an atmosphere of trust. Thus, it must be understood that the principal's self-evaluation should be shared with the teachers. In fairness to the process, the teachers' feedback cannot be anonymous. Anonymous responses only breed suspicion and undermine the goal of creating a climate of trust and transparency.

In the January/February 2016 issue of the *Harvard Business Review*, Detert and Burris argue that three serious risks occur when feedback is anonymous:

1. It reinforces the impression that it isn't safe to speak up openly.
2. It can set off a witch-hunt to find out who said what, leading away from the issues at hand.
3. It discourages the level of specificity that's needed to make real changes.[3]

Some teachers are sure to be anxious and fearful about signing their names to their responses. They would prefer to remain anonymous. Anonymity can be just as troubling to teachers when confronted with anonymous parent complaints. Nevertheless, some teachers will fear the possibility of some form of retribution if they make their name public. If this is prevalent, the principal must be sensitive to these fears and confront them openly with the faculty. Here is where the principal must exercise active listening and reflect understanding and empathy. By all means, avoid conveying that it is a silly and unwarranted fear. Rather, convey that it is an understandable fear and one that the principal and faculty can, working together, hope to resolve.

CLASSROOM CLIMATE SURVEYS

In addition to completing their own questionnaire, teachers are required to obtain feedback from students on the classroom climate (see appendix E). They are asked to distribute a classroom climate survey and share the results with their students and the principal. Climate surveys are designed to capture the intellectual, social, emotional, and physical experience a student encounters in the classroom. The classroom climate encompasses a mix of interactions that include student-to-teacher and student-to-student interactions, openness and receptivity, the size and makeup of the class, and the content and materials used.

Classroom climate surveys are readily available online and designed for various grade levels. They are easy to administer and best given twice a year, once at the end of the first quarter or semester and again near the end of the school year. Just as the principal must share his or her questionnaire responses with the teachers, teachers need to share students' responses with their classes.

DISTRICT CLIMATE SURVEYS

In addition to completing the classroom climate survey, it is a good idea to administer a district climate survey. According to a study conducted by Columbia University's Teachers College, climate surveys include norms, values, and expectations that reflect the extent to which people are feeling emotionally, socially, and physically safe, as well as engaged and respected.[4] The school climate includes spheres of school life that encompass safety, relationships, the quality of teaching and learning, and the school environment.

The results of the survey can reveal organizational patterns that reflect a healthy, shared, and cohesive vision or a climate that may be fragmented and harmful to the health of the organization. A Columbia Teachers College study revealed a growing gap between "school climate research, policy, practice, and teacher education." The study's review of the literature on school climate surveys indicated that a positive school climate is a good predictor of "academic achievement, school success, effective violence prevention, students' healthy development, and teacher retention."[5]

District climate surveys are readily available online and designed for various participants. They are easy to administer by hard copy or electronically. Many states have collaborated with local universities to construct reliable and valid climate surveys. They are best administered every two or three years.

STRENGTHS, WEAKNESSES, OPPORTUNITIES, AND THREATS (SWOT)

Rather than perform a district climate survey, a school district may prefer to complete an easy and quick analysis by using SWOT, a technique developed for industry and corporations. Participants in such an analysis are asked to identify the organization's strengths, weaknesses, opportunities, and threats. It is a good idea to solicit responses from the members of the board of education, teachers, administrators, and students. Once completed, the district can analyze the responses to compile the most frequent citations found in each category, which can in turn be used to construct district goals. SWOT analysis can also be used to pinpoint responses from a school's teachers and students, and construct school goals.

ORGANIZATIONAL CLIMATE

What is being asked of principals, superintendents, and teachers may be initially uncomfortable and, for some, an annoyance. In fact, the level of discomfort a principal experiences may be a good indication or measure of the health of the present organization and climate in the school district; however, once the principal, superintendent, and teachers experience the opportunity to listen to one another, the level of trust and collegiality is sure to improve.

As in all large social systems, there are sure to be a few outliers who fear being open and honest with their colleagues. They will either grudgingly comply or choose to leave. Nevertheless, resistance to change will always be present. Effective leaders are not easily deterred from challenging the status quo or making changes designed to improve learning conditions.

WORKING ALONE

Making systemic changes is a difficult task in a school organization. If principals are left to work alone, the position can lead to high levels of stress, which has resulted in frequent principal turnover in many school districts. When there is high turnover of principals, schools suffer a loss of leadership, and its effects are usually detrimental to students and faculty. Many school systems recognize the level of stress school principals encounter. In 2003, the New York City Public Schools were experiencing a turnover of principals every three years on average. As a response, they formed the not-for-profit New York City Leadership Academy, designed to support and better train principals.[6]

Since the 1990s, the research literature on the school principal's behavior has found that the most effective and successful principals are much more collaborative in the administration of their schools than their less-successful counterparts. These principals create opportunities for shared or distributive leadership, an approach supported by contemporary research on the behavior of effective school leaders. Furthermore, in light of how complex and demanding the position has become throughout the years, the research indicates that school systems have a responsibility to train principals to be collaborative leaders and support them in building effective learning communities.[7]

New York was greatly influenced by the work of the Wallace Foundation. With $1.5 billion in assets from the Wallaces, founders of *Reader's Digest*, the foundation turned its philanthropic work toward the study of practices and characteristics of effective school principals. After a decade of research and study, they suggested that effective principals engage in the following "Five Pivotal Practices That Shape Instructional Leadership":

1. Shaping a vision of academic success for all students based on high standards
2. Creating a climate hospitable to education so safety, a cooperative spirit, and other foundations of fruitful interaction prevail
3. Cultivating leadership in others so teachers and other adults assume their part in realizing the school vision
4. Improving instruction to enable teachers to teach at their best and students to learn at their utmost
5. Managing people, data, and processes to foster school improvement[8]

As is evident from the research literature, the practices cited here are widely and generally supported.

LEADERSHIP TEAMS

One of the essential components stressed by researchers is the building of leadership teams made up of teachers and administrators. Principals need more than the occasional workshop or pep talk to implement these teams. Thus, districts like New York City have begun to provide principals with trained professional coaches to work directly with them in their schools.

What is required of principals to be effective team leaders? Amy Edmondson, Novartis Professor of Leadership and Management at the Harvard Business School and renowned researcher in the formation of leadership teams, cites the following six attributes needed to be an effective team leader:

1. Be accessible and approachable
2. Invite participation
3. Acknowledge the limits of one's current knowledge
4. Display fallibility
5. Model curiosity
6. Frame the work of the team as a learning experience, rather than problems to be solved

She suggests that these behaviors can help the team feel psychologically safe and hence more likely to achieve creative and sustainable outcomes.[9] Principals possess many of these attributes and, with some help from trained coaches, are sure to become effective team leaders.

Granted, New York City is one of the largest school systems in the country and has many more resources to draw on than the majority of small rural and suburban districts, which may balk at the expense of leadership coaches. Nevertheless, school districts must provide their principals with quality support. If that function is valued and understood, districts will find the necessary funding to assign coaches to their school principals and assist them in forming leadership teams as a means of improving conditions for teaching and learning in their schools. With or without district support for coaches, the principals should do everything they can to establish teams in their schools.

RELATIONSHIP BETWEEN THE PRINCIPAL AND THE SUPERINTENDENT

Most superintendents struggle to supervise and fairly evaluate principals and at the same time provide them with strong support. That important responsibility competes with addressing the needs of the board of education, constructing the annual school budget, overseeing capital improvement plans, dealing with bond issues, and negotiating with collective bargaining units. Superintendents are tasked with handling such responsibilities, while also addressing the never-ending political issues that arrive at their doorstep.

Consumed by such responsibilities, superintendents rarely find enough time to spend with principals on their turf except to make occasional appearances at school plays, concerts, athletic events, and graduation exercises. This is routine and expected but much too far from the classrooms where instruction and learning take place.

Some superintendents, as a result of their involvement in professional organizations, encounter theories and research that can inform their practice and move them to find the time to visit the schools. The first change they usually make is to schedule visits to the schools in the district. Not every principal is thrilled to spend time in the school with the superintendent. Many find that such visits do little to improve their practice and simply take time away from their work.[10]

Principals should be clear on the purpose of the visit and collaborate with the superintendent to plan activities that will serve the needs of both. The school visit should be an opportunity for the principal and superintendent to share their respective observations of the teaching and learning that take place in the classrooms. Teachers should also understand the purpose and reason for such visits. The more interactions between the principal and the superintendent, as well as between the principal and the teachers and students, the more positive the professional relationships will become.

Some would argue that the interactions need to go beyond establishing professional relationships, but can they lead to better instruction and improved student performance? It would make for an interesting ethnographic study of the school climate and culture, and its impact on the performance of students. Nevertheless, it is difficult to track what the effects of a collaborative school environment would have on student achievement.

However, in theory and experience where there exists a high degree of collegiality and professional relationships among administrators and teachers, student learning is positively affected. Clearly, to be an effective supervisor, one must be approachable, present, and collaborative. It is a good idea for the principal and superintendent to occasionally have lunch with the teachers. Breaking bread with others is a long-standing and honored way to value everyone who sits at the table.

Another ethnographic exercise worth conducting, for it is a rich source of information, is to shadow a student for a day or follow a student's schedule during the school's open house. Some of these activities may sound contrived, but they flatten the hierarchy and diminish the perception of the superintendent and the principal as distant bosses, building a climate of trust. Without such efforts, the relationships between superintendent and principal, and principal and teachers, are hierarchical ones that operate based on positional power and rely on evaluation systems that focus on finding faults and weaknesses. It is important for supervisors to experience the negative response such value-loaded evaluation schemes provoke in those being supervised.

RELATIONSHIPS BETWEEN PRINCIPAL AND TEACHERS

The process being proposed is designed to enable principals to enhance their professional relationships with every key actor in their orbit. The more open and transparent the relationships are among the principal, superintendent, and teachers, the healthier the organization will be, and the students will be better served.

"The Principal Perspective," a 2012 report by the Center for Public Education, identified the difference between effective and ineffective principals. Effective principals provide support throughout the school year via ongoing and informal meetings with teachers. Rather than depending on infrequent formal evaluations to provide feedback to teachers, effective principals make frequent and spontaneous classroom visits and provide immediate feedback. Ineffective principals, on the other hand, make preplanned classroom visits and rarely provide follow-up feedback to teachers. The same can be said for superintendents.[11]

The findings presented in "The Principal Perspective" support the importance of frequent interactions and immediate feedback to those one supervises. Despite countless other responsibilities, superintendents cannot supervise principals from a distance, nor can principals supervise teachers if they rarely leave their offices. Just as superintendents must invest time to develop professional relationships with principals, principals must do the same with their teachers to be effective managers and true instructional leaders. They must communicate the importance of that function by making the focus of their supervision to "improve teacher performance, not merely cite deficits."

Effective supervision by administrators is the best means of exercising influence on the overall quality of instruction. It requires direct interaction with and observation of those with whom one works, along with a genuine commitment to enhancing the quality of services for the children in one's charge.

VOICES FROM THE FIELD

To gain an early reaction to use of the questionnaires, retired and practicing educators were approached. They included principals at every level, superintendents, teachers, and pupil personnel staff. Everyone spoke openly about how difficult it would be to flatten the traditional educational hierarchies they experienced. Their responses to the proposed process were not very promising. They thought that it was a noble idea but not likely to be acted on. They judged it to be highly idealistic and noted that with few exceptions, the principals they had worked with would not submit themselves to the process of being evaluated by their entire teaching staff.

In addition, they were skeptical of how superintendents and teachers would respond to being approached by principals suggesting that they share their self-evaluations. Furthermore, those who taught at the secondary level pointed out that they were evaluated by various supervisors assigned to their departments and thus had little interaction with their schools' principals.

BEST STRATEGY TO USE

Thus, in light of the solicited responses from retired and practicing educators, it might be best if the principal initially forgoes the proposed steps that include engaging their superintendent and teachers. The intent is to flatten the traditional school hierarchy, but although a noble and ideal endeavor, the steps proposed would require an extraordinary effort by the principal. Rather, it might be more realistic and manageable for the principal to begin by sharing their self-evaluation by means of the principal's questionnaire (see appendix A) with their school superintendent or immediate supervisor and not ask them to do the same. In addition, the principal, rather than seeking feedback from the entire school faculty, could begin the process by meeting with a group of formal and informal leaders in the school. Meeting with a smaller group to explain and discuss the intent and reasons behind the use of the principal's and teacher's questionnaires is more likely to result in open and honest feedback.

Soliciting input from the key voices in the system is ideal, but no longer requiring the superintendent and teachers to complete their questionnaires is a more practical approach to overcoming the fear of possible negative repercussions if they were to engage fully in the process. Moreover, it will take time to establish a level of trust in the process, and once the fears of the unknown are conquered, the voices of the superintendent and teachers are more likely to be heard through the self-evaluation process by means of the proposed questionnaires.

Throughout the process, the principals willing to engage in the process would be well served to keep the superintendent and other colleagues apprised of their efforts to "flatten the hierarchy" and how those efforts have been received. As others witness the positive results of seeking genuine constructive criticism from those one supervises, it will surely become easier in time to invite their active participation in the process.

PRINCIPALS' VOICES

In the summer of 2018, the National Principals Leadership Institute (NPLI) was convening its 21st weeklong gathering in New York City. The author, a former director of the institute, sought the organization's support and requested that the gathering's participants be asked to complete a survey. The purpose was to capture the voices of the principals in attendance, assess their willingness to engage fully in the self-evaluation process, and, if they were unwilling, determine why.

NPLI was kind enough to distribute the principal's questionnaire, a letter explaining its purpose, and the survey to the participants (appendix D) attending the organization's 2018 summer institute.[12] The institute attracted 105 principals from throughout the United States and Canada. Of that number, 54 completed the survey. In addition, nine principals other than those from the institute responded to the survey, for a total of 63 responses.

The Responses

Given the small sample size of the survey participants, it is hard to generalize based on the data collected. Nevertheless, the 63 responses received may well reflect the attitudes of suburban and urban principals. Based on those responses, principals are clearly willing to participate in the process of using the questionnaires as tools to enhance the climate in their schools even though they do not have a similar process in place in their districts.

Of the 63 respondents, 18 were from suburban districts and 44 from urban districts. The field for district type was left blank in one survey. The responses to the six survey questions were as follows:

1. *"Would you complete the questionnaire and participate in the process?"* Seventy-six percent of the principals, 16 suburban and 31 urban, answered yes.
2. *"Did you find the questionnaire to fairly reflect the work and challenges principals encounter?"* Ninety percent found the questionnaire to reflect their work, with seven urban principals responding somewhat and two responding no. Fourteen of the suburban principals found it to reflect their work, with only one no and one somewhat.
3. *"Do you have a similar process in place in your district?"* Fifty-eight percent answered no. Only seven suburban and 19 urban principals answered yes.
4. *"Would your superintendent participate in the process?"* Forty-eight percent answered yes, which included eight suburban and 21 urban principals. Six suburban principals said no, and two indicated that the process would need modifications. Nine urban principals

said no, with 10 indicating there would need to be some modifications.
5. *"Would your teachers subscribe to the process?"* Fifty-nine percent answered yes, which included 12 suburban and 25 urban principals. Six principals said they were not sure.
6. *"Do you have leadership teams in your school?"* Ninety-five percent of the surveyed principals answered yes. Two answered no, and one said it would require modifications.

Several urban principals noted that they do not report directly to the superintendent and instead report to a deputy or district supervisor; however, 59 percent of the principals reported that their teachers would participate in the process, which was significantly higher than the percentage of principals who thought their superintendents would participate.

A few commented that they would participate only if the process were to replace their current evaluation system. Some indicated that their districts' surveys were time consuming and not very effective. Several noted that their teachers' unions would have to agree to participate and might not willingly do so.

Although based on only a small sampling of principals, the results of the survey indicate that many districts do not use such a process and that there may be a need for a process designed to promote a more collegial and transparent school organization. Furthermore, it was evident that the majority of the principals surveyed were willing to be more open and transparent. In light of the reported doubts about the willingness of superintendents and teachers to participate, principals seeking to implement the questionnaire process will most likely have to take the initiative. It will surely be a test of their leadership skills.

WHY DO IT?

The professional development and evaluation requirements bombarding schools are overwhelming, demeaning, and ineffective. Existing evaluation practices do little to create an open and honest exchange between professionals and improve teaching and learning. Rather, they have led to high rates of principal and teacher turnover fueled by an unrealistic overload of work that results in frustration and, ultimately, burnout.

According to a study reported in *Education Week* on August 3, 2018, significant turnover of principals has continued. The article cites a 2015 report by the School Leaders Network, which estimated that 25 percent of principals left their schools each year, and almost half left in the third year. That rate of turnover can only result in negative academic and financial consequences.[13]

The response from the majority of principals completing the survey was that they are willing and ready to risk opening themselves up to what may be at first painful and often unjust criticism of their performance. Uncomfortable as the first steps may be, they recognize that unless there is a culture of trust in which everyone works cooperatively to improve their performance, real improvement is not likely to take place. Likewise, it will take courage and persistence on the part of principals to approach those who supervise them, but implementing an open and transparent process is sure to enhance their leadership skills and improve the quality of the public schools they administer.

NOTES

1. The superintendent's questionnaire is based on a survey conducted by the National School Public Relations Association. See Louise Henry et al., "Characteristics of Effective Superintendents," *National School Public Relations Association*, 2005, https://www.nspra.org/files/docs/CharacteristicsOfEffectiveSuperintendents.pdf.

2. The principal's questionnaire is based on "Highly Effective Principals," *National Association of Secondary School Principals*, last modified November 7, 2013, https://www.nassp.org/policy-advocacy-center/nassp-position-statements/highly-effective-principals/.

3. James R. Detert and James R. Burris, "Can Your Employees Really Speak Freely?" *Harvard Business Review*, January/February 2016, https://hbr.org/2016/01/can-your-employees-really-speak-freely.

4. Gillian Kiley, "School Environment Key to Retaining Teachers, Promoting Student Achievement," *Phys.org*, October 26, 2016, https://phys.org/news/2016-10-school-environment-key-retaining-teachers.html#jCp.

5. Jonathan Cohen et al., "School Climate: Research, Policy, and Teacher Education," *Teachers College Record* 111, no. 1 (January 2009): 181.

6. New York Leadership Academy: contactus@nycleaddershipacademy.org.

7. "The Principal Perspective: At a Glance," *Center for Public Education*, last modified April 2012, http://www.centerforpubliceducation.org/research/principal-perspective-glance.

8. Pamela Mendels, "The Effective Principal: Five Pivotal Practices That Shape Instructional Leadership," *JSD* 33, no. 1 (2012).

9. Amy C. Edmondson, "Managing the Risk of Learning: Psychological Safety in Work Teams," in *International Handbook of Organizational Teamwork and Cooperative*

Working, ed. Michael A. West, Dean Tjosvold, and Ken G. Smith (London: Wiley, 2003), 255–76.

10. John Fitzsimons, "The Struggle to Supervise Principals," *School Administrator* 73, no. 6 (June 2016): 12.

11. "The Principal Perspective: At a Glance," *Center for Public Education*, last modified April 2012, http://www.centerforpubliceducation.org/research/principal-perspective-glance.

12. Denisa R. Superville, "Most Principals Like Their Jobs: Here's What Makes Them Change Schools or Quit," *Education Week*, August 3, 2018, blogs.edweek.org/edweek/District_Dossier/2018/08/principal_job_satisfaction_turnover_tenure.html.

13. Superville, "Most Principals Like Their Jobs."

TWO

Surviving

Becoming an Effective and Resilient Leader

We only think when confronted with a problem. —John Dewey

Horace Mann should be no stranger to principals. His work in establishing the need for public schools should be understood and appreciated. After all, the position of principal emerged from that of the lead, or "principal," teacher in the school. Although principals have had little influence on the governance and funding of public schools, they must have a thorough understanding of how schools are funded, as well as the politics of school funding.

The governance and funding processes in place in the United States have real consequences for public schools throughout the country. Although such processes are distant from the principal's day-to-day work, principals need to be well informed as to how they function. After all, knowing how public schools are funded and governed can prove beneficial to principals, especially when they are seeking essential resources and challenging those in control.

GOVERNANCE

Unlike in many smaller countries, where education is overseen by a national ministry of education, in the United States, the primary responsibility for educating children rests with the states. Although each state has different wording in its constitution, they all clearly express their obligation to provide a thorough and efficient education to school-age children. A principal should be familiar with the language in his or her state's constitution regarding the state's obligations to support and maintain its public schools. Each state has established a department of education to oversee its public schools, which are in turn governed by county or local community boards of education. The one exception is Hawaii, where there is one state board appointed by the governor and no regional or local school boards or superintendents.

The state education departments can be either very helpful and a good resource for the local school districts or intrusive and disruptive. It is not uncommon to experience a high turnover of state commissioners, which further exacerbates problems within the districts they serve. Many states have elected state superintendents and local boards of education. In some cities, the mayor appoints the board members.

The more turnover of board members, be they elected or appointed, the more likely there will be negative consequences for the school district. One such consequence is a high turnover of school superintendents and school principals. The more stable the board, the lower turnover of administrators.

FUNDING

Every state relies on a combination of tax revenues to fund their public schools, but the primary source of revenue is derived from property taxes. Therein lies a significant problem over which principals have little control beyond their ability to seek out a position in a wealthy community or state that provides adequate funding and remains committed to providing sufficient resources to its public schools. Indeed, the reliance on property taxes has created substantial inequities in school districts throughout the country.

Such inequities have caused tremendous challenges in poorer school districts throughout the United States. A lack of adequate funding has left schools devoid of essential resources, especially the resources required to establish healthy social and emotional learning environments, a must in such districts. According to the U.S. Census Bureau, the average per-pupil expenditure in the United States was $11,762 in 2016; however, spending varies widely among the country's school districts. New York City, the largest school district by enrollment, spent $24,109 per pupil in

2016, while Baltimore County, the sixth-largest district, spent $13,512 per pupil.[1]

Such variations are to some extent attributable to the cost of living differences throughout the nation. More important, however, is the way in which per-pupil spending reflects how much those in power value public education and fulfill their obligation to provide schools with more than just adequate funding, which is in turn used to pay for such crucial operating expenses as staffing, supplies, and the maintenance of buildings and grounds.

As a result of the political decisions made by those in power, the gap between poor and wealthy communities continues to grow. State funding formulas have been tinkered with for decades, and commissions have periodically formed to study equitable ways of funding schools. No commission has been able to arrive at a reasonable solution.

SEEKING EDUCATIONAL EQUITY

Many groups have been formed to seek adequate school funding throughout the country, particularly following the 1973 Supreme Court decision in *San Antonio Independent School District v. Rodriguez*. The case concerned the school-funding system in place in Texas, which was based on property taxes and created substantial inequities between rich and poor districts. In a 5–4 decision, the Supreme Court ruled that the remedy rested with the state, and Texas could continue with its existing method of funding schools.[2]

Appeals to the state court challenging a state's failure to fund its public schools adequately took place in the majority of U.S. states in the decades following the 1973 Supreme Court ruling. Although such challenges initially saw little success, later court actions proved promising. According to Michael A. Rebell, executive director of the Center for Educational Equity at Teachers College, Columbia University, plaintiffs prevailed in eight of the 17 cases filed in state supreme courts between 2009 and June 2017.[3]

In some rulings, however, the courts cited the plaintiffs for failing to distribute their funding equitably at the local level to ensure that students received the necessary funds for an adequate education. They noted, for example, that in some districts athletic programs and facilities received adequate funding while buildings crumbled, class sizes increased, and staffing remained insufficient.[4] To ensure equitable funding, principals must work hand and glove with their central administration to budget wisely and judiciously.

Moving state powerbrokers to establish fair and equitable funding for schools under their jurisdiction is not likely to succeed as long as there continues to be local control of the school district. Wealthy communities will continue to provide greater resources to their students than poorer districts. These are crucial challenges facing every school. The need to compete for scarce resources is a reality confronted by every school principal.

SEPARATION OF CHURCH AND STATE

School funding likewise becomes a key issue when there are significant shifts in the demographics of the school's community, as notably occurred in the Lawrence, New York, public school district. During a 20-year period from approximately 1991 to 2011, the district's student enrollment shrank from more than 6,000 students to less than 3,000 as Orthodox Jewish families moved into the district. Attendance at religious schools expanded to more than 5,000 resident students. The Orthodox Jewish members of the community did not send their children to Lawrence's public schools.

According to the Education Commission of the States in the February 2012 report "State Aid to Nonpublic Schools," transportation aid to nonpublic schools is granted in 29 states. Policies regarding aid for nonpublic schools obligated Lawrence to provide transportation to children attending private or parochial schools, if the school was within a 15-mile radius of the child's home. Transportation costs can be significant in communities in which many residents send their children to private and parochial schools. For example, Lawrence spent almost $10 million on transporting nonpublic students to and from school, the majority of them to yeshivas.

In addition to transportation services, the commission reported that 21 states require that public schools provide textbooks and learning benefits to every child attending nonpublic schools. Lastly, the report noted that some states, including New York, require their public schools' learning benefits to include services to every child with learning disabilities, as well as all social services. Such expenditures, when permitted or required by the state, drain resources from public schools. As a result of the aid to the nonpublic schools in Lawrence, the per-pupil expenditures ballooned to more than $30,000 per pupil, the highest in the state, and led to ongoing budget defeats.

Lawrence may be a unique example, but it aptly demonstrates the unnecessary burden the laws in support of funding education in nonpublic schools place on public schools. The private and parochial school lobbies are alive and well in Albany, just as they are in many state capitals. There remains little separation of church and state when it comes to school funding, and the outlook is grim.

In a 2017 decision by the U.S. Supreme Court, the justices further weakened the separation of church and state when they ruled 7–2 that a Lutheran church was eligible to receive a state grant to repair its school's playground, raising further questions about the public funding of religious organizations.[5] To add further insult, in her first official trip to New York City in 2018, U.S. secretary of education Betsy DeVos declined to visit any of the public schools she represented as secretary. Instead, the secretary chose to tour two Orthodox Jewish schools, the Manhattan School for Girls and the Yeshiva Darchei Torah. She ended her visit by meeting with the archbishop of New York and other Catholic leaders.[6]

Such events, along with the pressure to open more and more public charter schools, are all the more reason for public school principals to organize with school board members, superintendents, parents, community leaders, and teacher unions to oppose the siphoning off of taxpayers' dollars for the aid of private and parochial schools. Principals should not discount the political capital they possess with local, state, and federal officials, and their ability to make their voices heard in their state houses and congressional offices.

POLITICAL INFLUENCE AND LOCAL CONTROL

It might be helpful for principals to think of the political system in place as a series of six concentric circles and know which circle they occupy. The first, outermost circle is occupied by the state legislators; the second circle contains the state department of education and an appointed educational commissioner; the third circle is occupied by the local county or community board of education; the fourth circle contains the superintendent of schools charged with overseeing the district; the fifth circle is occupied by the principal, who supervises the school; and the sixth, innermost circle represents the classroom and contains the students and teachers.

Ideally, every occupant of each circle has the same mission and purpose: to provide a thorough and efficient public education to all children. Yet, principals have been consistently asked to undertake a number of reforms by those most distant from the classrooms. Unfortunately, such individuals have an inordinate amount of influence and power over what takes place in the schoolhouse. Politicians do not hesitate to cross boundaries and penetrate deep into the school system, either with costly reforms or severe budget restrictions.

Public education, funded by tax dollars, cannot avoid being embroiled in state and local politics. As a result, principals and teachers, occupying positions far from those in power, are often ignored and deemed inconsequential. When those in political power cut school funding and impose questionable school reforms, it is the principals and teachers who are forced to deal with the consequences. What, then, can a principal do to be heard in such a political environment?

Principals should be active members in local, state, and national professional organizations and their unions. In numbers, there is strength and political influence; however, principal and teacher organizations are often criticized as being interested only in their own well-being, at the expense of children. To counter that perception, principals must also become politically aware and engaged with their communities. One way for principals to counter distant political forces is to establish good relationships with local parents, who pay state and local taxes, and whose votes for state legislators and local boards of education can influence those in the outermost circles.

National organizations formed around the various academic disciplines, for example, the National Council of Teachers of English (NCTE) and the National Council for the Social Studies (NCSS), have had extensive influence on instructional practice and curriculum development; however, although large in size, they have had little impact on state legislators or the state departments of education. Organizations representing principals, for instance, the National Association of Secondary School Principals (NASSP) and the National Association of Elementary Principals (NAEP), have likewise focused more on improving curriculum, instructional practice, and leadership practices than on influencing state law.

On the other hand, such large national educational organizations as the National Education Association (NEA), National School Boards Association (NSBA), and American Federation of Teachers (AFT) have the size and funding to lobby legislators at both the state and federal levels. Politicians are quick to seek their endorsements when campaigning for office. Once elected, however, there is no guarantee that a politician will support policies advocated by those groups.

One possible educational alliance that may prove influential—and in which principals should be thoroughly engaged—is that of higher education and the public schools. The goal would be to promote educational practices that are based on sound teaching and learning research rather than political expediency. Such partnerships will not arise unless public-school principals reach out to their colleagues in higher education. Many principals might find that local institutions of higher learning would welcome the opportunity to have their schools serve as lab schools. Unlike attempts to create business/school partnerships, educational partnerships are more likely to serve the genuine needs of the schools than to put money in the pockets of businesses and corporations.

University and school partnerships exist. For example, New York University established a Mindful Education Lab, housed within the Metropolitan Center for Research on Equity and the Transformation of Schools. The lab examines the impacts of mindfulness on teacher effectiveness and student learning, and offers training in mindfulness techniques for students, teachers, and administrators in New York City public schools. The Teachers College at Columbia University offers similar programs. They serve to enhance curriculum and instruction but as of yet have not served to influence state educational policies. Nonetheless, the outlook for such partnerships is promising.

SUPPORT FOR TEACHER LABOR UNIONS

Political action among teachers appeared to be at a new high in 2018, as teachers throughout the country marched on the state houses, demanding that their legislators not violate their sworn oaths to fund public schools fully.[7] In addition to going on strike to fight for higher wages and protest against cuts to school funding, teachers throughout the United

States took further action by pursuing political office. As reported by *Education Week*, by September 2018, more than 150 teachers had filed to run for state legislative positions, particularly in states in which large teacher strikes took place.[8]

Yet, despite such political engagement on the part of teachers, membership in teacher unions is on the decline. According to the 2015–2016 Survey of Teachers and Principals, membership in teacher unions fell to 69 percent from 79 percent in 2011–2012. The U.S. Bureau of Labor Statistics reported an overall decline in union membership from 20.1 percent to 11.1 percent in the United States between 1983 and 2015.[9] Furthermore, the 2018 decision by the U.S. Supreme Court in *Janus v. AFCME* to revoke a 40-year precedent that required nonunion employees to pay union dues does not bode well for teacher unions. Given that a sizeable number of teachers claim they are not in agreement with their unions' positions, the court ruled that they should not be compelled to fund what they oppose. The court concluded, "Because the compelled subsidization of private speech seriously impinges on First Amendment rights, it cannot be casually allowed."[10]

Principals must remain strong and active union members in this period of decline, and they should lend their visible and vocal support to teacher unions as they fight for reasonable salaries and benefits. The teaching process is damaged when the relationship between the administration and the faculty becomes one of management verses labor. Students and parents are best served when there is a high degree of collegiality among the teachers and the administration. If situations have reached a breaking point in a principal's district, he or she might even want to consider running for the state legislature.

BUILDING A PROFESSIONAL LEARNING COMMUNITY IN THE SCHOOL

Why is it that when the economy is suffering and funding for public education is being capped or cut, superintendents often are quick to reduce the professional development budget? What message is that sending to the district's faculty and students? Does preservice education and training, regardless of the institution awarding the degree or the state granting the certificate, guarantee quality instruction and excellent pupil services? Do academic degrees and state certifications ensure that quality instruction and services will be consistently delivered by new teachers, as well as classroom veterans?

No principal is naïve enough to give too much weight to academic degrees and state certification processes. To the contrary, principals recognize the serious limitations of preservice education. They are fully aware that training is no guarantee that teachers will emerge ready to enter the classroom with the necessary skills to be effective educators. Principals know that continuous improvement in performance requires ongoing professional development. Serious professional development cannot take place during a scheduled day or two of in-service activities.

Principals understand that it is essential for every educator, novice or experienced, to engage in planned, ongoing professional development to remain current in their fields and adapt to an ever-changing society; however, principals who profess such beliefs send mixed or contradictory messages when they first look to staff training as a place to cut spending.

No one disputes the importance of the professional staff. Their value is readily apparent in their cost. Salaries and benefits represent 70 percent of most public-school budgets. Schools are, after all, labor-intensive enterprises. Yet, if the most-valued and expensive resources are the school system's professionals, why do most school districts invest so little in their continued professional development?

How much, for example, would it cost to provide each member of the professional staff with membership in a professional organization that could enhance his or her work assignment? Many school districts provide the superintendent and administrators with paid membership in professional organizations of their choosing as a contract provision. Why shouldn't the same provision be available to all professional staff

COSTS AND BENEFITS

To assess the viability of providing each member of the professional staff with a membership in a relevant professional organization, it may be helpful to calculate the cost and the potential benefits. The average cost of professional membership in an organization like NCTE or the National Council of Teachers of Mathematics (NCTM) is approximately $100 and includes a subscription to the organization's professional journal.

Assuming that three hundred professionals are employed in the district, the district need budget only $30,000 to ensure that each staff member is a member of a professional organization aligned with his or her assignments and responsibilities. If salaries and benefits cost an average of $60,000, for a total of $18 million, the expenditure of $30,000 for professional memberships is a small price to pay, representing only 0.17 percent of the total cost of salaries and benefits.

As part of the process, staff members could be responsible for identifying the most beneficial national professional organization, one that would not only meet their needs, but also enhance instruction for their students. Discussing the benefits of being affiliated with various professional organizations is a powerful professional development activity for teachers. Membership in professional organizations also gives teachers access to the latest professional literature, which could be shared and discussed at grade-level and department meetings.

With 100 percent of the professional staff affiliated with appropriate professional groups, the stage will be set for ongoing professional development. The activities generated by such affiliations far surpass the perfunctory two or three days of scheduled in-service programs. In addition, such an initiative sends a strong message to all employees that they are respected and valued professionals.[11]

Principals can further enhance professional development by approaching the relevant unions and suggesting that they share in the cost of some professional development activities. Unions can play an active role in selecting the appropriate memberships, as well as planning and conducting in-service activities. No such collaboration and cooperation is likely to take place when the first thing to be cut in tough economic times is the staff development budget.

LEARNING COMMUNITIES

If a district wants to build a true learning community in its schools, principals must display a strong commitment to the ongoing professional development of the staff. Otherwise, the district risks becoming a group of loosely affiliated schools tied to rigid protocols, resisting change no matter how questionable their current practices. Systemic improvements based on sound educational research are not likely to take place in such an environment.

Schools are continually challenged by professional isolation, which develops when few opportunities exist for teachers and support staff to observe one another's work and share in the discovery of best practices. Chances for reflection, analysis, and discussion with trusted colleagues are limited. Supporting quality in-service programs and attendance at state and national workshops and conferences will pay dividends in improved instruction and services to students if teachers incorporate and refine their practice when they return to their classrooms.

Teachers rarely see one another teach. Elementary teachers are with their self-contained classes for the entire day except when their classes are scheduled for music, art, or physical education. No time is set aside for them to observe one another's work. Typically a secondary teacher is scheduled to teach five or six classes per day, along with a preparation period. The generally accepted practice is that no time has been set aside for them as well to observe one another's work. Teachers work in isolation, unlike what is found in other professions, where collaboration and problem solving are expected and a common practice. If principals were to build into a teacher's schedule, they would have opportunities to see one another teach and have the time to talk about their work.

Professional development does not guarantee immediate results or changes in teacher or student behaviors, but without it, ineffective practices go unchallenged. If principals want to serve as instructional leaders, they must courageously promote budgets that include funds to support the professional growth of the entire staff.

NOTES

1. Stephen Wheeler, "Census Shows Where Public School Dollars Go," *U.S. Census Bureau*, June 4, 2018, https://www.census.gov/library/stories/2018/06/school-spending.html. See also Joel McFarland et al., *The Condition of Education 2018* (Washington, DC: National Center for Education Statistics, 2018), https://nces.ed.gov/pubs2018/2018144.pdf.

2. "San Antonio Independent School District v. Rodriguez," *Oyez*, https://www.oyez.org/cases/1972/71-1332.

3. Michael A. Rebell, "Courts and Kids: Pursuing Educational Equity Through the State Courts; 2017 Supplement," 2017, http://schoolfunding.info/wp-content/uploads/2017/07/COURTS-AND-KIDS-2017-Supplement.-07.12.17-.pdf.

4. Rebell, "Courts and Kids."

5. Richard Wolf, "Supreme Court Declares Churches Eligible for Some Public Funds," *USA Today*, June 28, 2017, https://www.usatoday.com/story/news/politics/2017/06/26/supreme-court-declares-churches-eligible-public-funds/102438402/.

6. Denis Slattery and Molly Crane-Newman, "Betsy DeVos Visits Yeshivas in NYC but Skips Public Schools," *New York Daily News*, May 16, 2018, http://www.

nydailynews.com/new-york/education/betsy-devos-visits-yeshivas-nyc-skips-public-schools-article-1.3993828.

7. Madeline Will, "Teacher Strikes Are Heating Up in More States," *Education Week*, September 12, 2018, https://www.edweek.org/ew/articles/2018/09/12/teacher-strikes-are-heating-up-in-more.html.

8. "Over 150 Teachers Are Running for State Office. Here's What We Know about Them," *Education Week*, September 27, 2018, https://www.edweek.org/ew/section/multimedia/teachers-running-for-state-office.html.

9. Megan Dunn and James Walker, "Union Membership in the United States," *U.S. Bureau of Labor Statistics*, last modified September 2016, https://www.bls.gov/spotlight/2016/union-membership-in-the-united-states/home.htm.

10. Brian Miller, "Unpacking the Janus Decision," *Forbes*, June 27, 2018, https://www.forbes.com/sites/briankmiller/2018/06/27/unpacking-the-janus-decision/#290a0afd41a4.

11. John Fitzsimons, "Connecting Our Staff to Their Professional Affiliations," *School Administrator* 69, no. 6 (June 2012): 16–17.

THREE
Collaborating
The Role of Central Office

> Education is not preparation for life; education is life itself.
> —John Dewey

In the vast majority of school districts, the central office encompasses numerous essential personnel, in addition to the superintendent. Except for small school districts, most central offices are also staffed with an assistant superintendent and a business manager. In larger systems, there are district curriculum coordinators. Large urban or county systems are also staffed with area or multiple deputy or assistant superintendents who report to a chancellor or county superintendent. Much like superintendents, however, such personnel can become tied down with a good deal of administrative minutiae and rarely visit the schools they support.

It is important that principals establish close working relationships with the central office staff and insist on them conducting scheduled visits to their schools. One way to ensure their presence in the school is to place them frequently on the agenda of meetings of the leadership team and faculty. If a superintendent fails to insist on the presence of central office support personnel in the schools, principals must pick up the phone and invite them. Everyone likes to feel that they are important and needed. Central office staff can provide principals with significant support and need not be called on only when there is a crisis.

It is not unusual for the central office to remain at a distance from their schools out of respect and appreciation for the principals' need for some degree of autonomy. No one in a leadership position wants to be oversupervised or closely monitored. What is suggested here is that there be a balanced collegial and respectful working relationship between the principal and the central office, rather than remaining distant, isolated, and impersonal.

VISIBLE PRESENCE

Principals may be familiar with the notion of "Management by Wandering Around" (MBWA), a concept popular in the leadership literature. They can easily incorporate that approach by walking through the halls and into classrooms, with or without the superintendent and at times with various members of the central office staff. Such a practice provides a good opportunity to see the work of teachers and students firsthand and share observations. It can prove to be instructive for all parties.

While the MBWA approach may at first create a little anxiety in the faculty and staff, if exercised frequently enough, it will come to be viewed as routine practice. Principals must be sure to explain that those visits are intended to support and enhance the work of teaching and learning, and are not for the purpose of conducting formal or informal evaluations or performance reviews.

Principals initially may find team visits to be awkward, but, in time, they will soon become comfortable with the process, as will the teachers. The visits provide an opportunity to share observations, insights, and research on best practices with the superintendent, central office administrators, and faculty. The more present the central office staff is in the school, the more positive the professional relationships between faculty and staff will become. As a sign of their willingness to learn and grow, principals must convey a genuine openness to accepting support and insights from the central office staff. That openness also conveys a principal's confidence and personal security in his or her position.

Superintendents and central office personnel cannot provide effective support to principals from a distance. To influence the overall quality of instruction, they must establish close working relationships with school principals, make direct observations of each principal's work, and demonstrate a genuine commitment to enhancing the quality of their instructional leadership and overall administrative skills. Principals should encourage such interactions rather than take false comfort in remaining isolated in their schools. The resulting synergism is powerful and rewarding for everyone involved.

The central administrators, especially the superintendent, need not be strangers to principals and their staffs. Removing the barrier between the central office administrators and the faculty and students in the schools will help to build a more cohesive system, as well as improve its overall effectiveness; however, such a change is not likely to happen without the initiative of the principals. Strong and confident principals are always looking for resources to help them improve their schools. They exhibit a confidence that enables them to open wide their schoolhouse doors.

TRANSFORMING THE CENTRAL OFFICE

Commissioned by the Wallace Foundation and published in 2010, by the Center for the Study of Teaching and Policy at the University of Washington, the report *Central Office Transformation for District-Wide Teaching and Learning Improvement* made valuable contributions to the ongoing discussion of the role and purpose of the central office. In the study documented in the report, researchers studied the central office operations in three large urban districts: Atlanta, Georgia; New York, New York; and Oakland, California.[1]

The leaders in those school systems recognized that districts are not able to improve teaching and learning without substantial support from the central office. Making improvements in those areas requires the central office to change its focus radically, decreasing its emphasis on administrative functions, and demonstrate a commitment to improving the quality of instruction by working hand-in-hand with school principals.

In the districts featured in the study, staff members engaged in the transformation by first examining their current practice and then determining what changes they would need to make to support the school administrators more effectively. The districts incorporated the following five transformational dimensions:

1. Developing partnerships with the school principals to improve instructional leadership practices
2. Providing trained support personnel known as instructional leadership directors, assigned to work directly with the school principals

3. Reorganizing the central office staff to ensure they are contributing to supporting improvements in teaching and learning
4. Moving from the role of central oversight to that of "stewardship," engaging in ongoing development of a theory of action required for sustaining the central office transformation
5. Engaging in the collection of student performance data to inform practice, not document failure

The report concluded with four recommendations. The first was to change the focus of the central office from that of a distant group of strangers providing bureaucratic support for functions far removed from instructional practice. The second recommendation was to start the transformational process by developing action plans tied to the context of improving teaching and learning. The third recommendation was to invest in adding trained coaching staff, designated as instructional leadership directors (ILDs), to provide direct support to the school principals and serve as the interface between the central office and the school. The final recommendation was to be sure that every stakeholder in the system, as well as external political forces, understand the need to change the focus and functions of the central office administrators.

Although not specifically mentioned in the recommendations, the most crucial stakeholder that needs to be supportive and aware of the changes from the start is the board of education. The report likewise did not mention the need for the superintendent or chancellor to be spearheading the changes in the central office operations. Superintendents and chancellors must examine their traditional leadership roles in the operation and oversight of the central office and insist that the focus be on improving the quality of teaching and learning. Doing so should be part of every superintendent's agenda as well as on the agenda of such key administrators as the business administrator and personnel director.

THE STATUS QUO

Yes, the districts involved in the study were all large urban districts, which may give principals in smaller suburban and rural districts reason to pause and struggle with its relevance; however, it is most likely that their central offices function in a traditional fashion, and the central office personnel are rarely seen in the school buildings, except when invited to see school plays or participate in moving-up or graduation ceremonies.

Principals can initiate change if they begin by addressing the need for more support from central office with their superintendents, or they can choose to "go along to get along" and not challenge the status quo.

Some principals may even welcome the lack of central office presence in their schools, because when central office staff do appear, they just take the principals away from their routine tasks. Their view is that school visits are more bothersome than helpful. They may be right, if their superintendents and central offices have continued to operate in the traditional manner of being concerned about regulations, adherence to policies, and general administrative minutiae. If the central office has yet to begin to exercise any of the five transformational dimensions noted in the 2010 report, and no action plans tied to teaching and learning have been constructed, such sentiments among principals are well understood.

Nevertheless, if a principal finds herself or himself in a situation in which interactions with the superintendent and the central office administrators are limited or nonexistent, the principal will need to take the initiative to suggest a better way to operate. Since the central office controls funding sources and how they are distributed to the schools, the chance of being supported by an assigned ILD is slim. Here is where the principal needs to push hard to initiate transformational changes designed to focus on the quality of instruction.

ENCOURAGING PROFESSIONAL GROWTH

Although superintendents in large districts may not have sufficient time to spend at each school, they do have support staff that can. In New York, for example, there are district superintendents assigned to the elementary and middle school in community districts, as well as high school district superintendents, all under the direction of the school's chancellor. No matter how small or large the school district is, the mission of the central office is to improve the quality of instruction in all of the schools in the district. To succeed in that mission, they must provide sufficient resources and support to the school principals and to the schools.

Those who occupy positions in the central office are well aware that principals will benefit from interacting with colleagues. It is easy for principals to feel isolated from one another, and they will seek informal contacts with one another throughout the year. Monthly administrative council meetings do serve to bring them together, but in those situations, the agenda is usually that of the superintendent and is filled with items concerning day-to-day operations and general administrative issues.

Administrative retreats—if conducted over several days, off-site, and when school is not in session—can be powerful professional development experiences for a district's administrators. The better retreats involve advanced planning by a committee of administrators and should be tied to the district's goals. If appropriate, an outside facilitator may be helpful in leading discussion about controversial topics. All in all, retreats serve as periods of concentrated time in which central office administrators and principals can enhance professional and personal relationships, the elements essential to building a strong administrative team.

Principals also will benefit greatly from holding active memberships in state and national professional organizations. Superintendents should promote such affiliations and ensure that the district professional development budget provides sufficient funds to cover the costs of those memberships. Memberships that should be held by all principals include memberships in the Association for Supervision and Curriculum Development (ASCD) and the American Educational Research Association (AERA).

Elementary principals should be active members of the National Association of Elementary School Principals (NAESP). Secondary principals should hold active memberships in the National Association of Secondary School Principals (NASSP). The district should pay for all such memberships, and, if necessary, memberships should be a benefit included in the principals' employment contracts. Principals will also benefit from the Yearbook of the National Society for the Study of Education (NSSE). Although publication ended in 2009, the yearbooks are a major source of outstanding research and insights on crucial issues in education and can be found in most public libraries.[2]

Today's principals are under a good deal of stress, given the scope and responsibilities of the office. Thus, it is imperative that principals remain in good physical condition. The superintendent should encourage principals to participate in regular exercise programs. If possible, superintendents should provide them with access to the high school fitness facilities and urge them to use those facilities whenever possible. Some schools have formed running and walking clubs as well offering yoga and meditation classes for district employees. The central administration can play a major role in supporting such activities by providing the necessary resources to the staff.

PUPIL PERSONNEL SUPPORT

One of the most challenging areas for principals is providing appropriate services to children with learning disabilities, be they mild or severe. Here is where the pupil personnel services director (PPSD), a key central office position, can provide essential support to the principal and teachers. From referral procedures to out-of-district placements, they must ensure that sensible policies are in place and conform to the laws and regulations related to the Individuals with Disabilities Education Act (IDEA).

Sensible is the operative word. Identifying children with mild disabilities that can be interfering with a child's learning can be difficult for teachers. Teachers will need training to recognize children with a possible learning disability who need to be referred for an evaluation. Evaluations are time consuming and will require the input of the classroom teacher and the principal. If appropriate, they are necessary and justified. Yet, if they are inappropriate, they place inordinate demands on the principal and special education staff. Consequently, teachers need suitable training to identify the signs of a learning disability in their students.

Here too, for example, is where principals can use the support of the PPSD. The number of referrals and evaluations need to be tracked and analyzed by the director, and, when necessary, corrective action is required. In addition, the director must be sure that the individual educational plan (IEP) constructed does not make unreasonable demands on the child, the classroom teachers, or special education staff. Unless there exists a close working relationship between the school principal and the PPSD, special education services may be more disruptive than productive.

CURRICULUM SUPPORT

Principals at any level can use the support of curriculum experts. The central office, under the leadership of the superintendent, must ensure that aligned and coherent curriculum documents exist and personnel are ensuring that they are being implemented in the schools. At the elementary level, the focus is on literacy and numeracy skills. Here, reading consultants have traditionally supported principals. To be literate, one needs not only to read but also to write. There has been a concerted effort to provide greater balance to the language arts curriculum by having students writing, as well as reading and comprehending. Writing as a process was the new buzzword and was introduced at every level of education.

More progressive districts, with the support of their central administration, have provided support to elementary and middle school principals in the form of literacy coaches and math coaches. Such coaches were assigned to work closely with classroom teachers to model best practices and keep teachers abreast of the latest and most effective ways of teaching their subjects. Many literacy coaches emerged from the ranks of reading teachers. The math coaches were recruited from within the schools from those teachers who had a strong format background in mathematics and the skills to work side by side with their colleagues.

Curriculum alignment and support at the secondary levels traditionally was the responsibility of department chairs or district supervisors. Here, the central office plays a key oversight role in ensuring that the curriculum is aligned with the state standards and implemented properly in each subject area. Principals at the secondary level can easily fall into thinking that all is well with the curriculum that is listed in the program of studies in the student handbook.

High school principals are frequently challenged in confronting the complexities of most secondary curricula, with the number of the required and elective offerings. To make matters worse, many course offerings are either standard, honors, or advanced placement courses. If that is not enough, there is also the ever-present pressure to add more differentiations or make radical changes. For example, with the addition of such now-popular initiatives as science, technology, engineering, and mathematics (STEM) programs, and the enhanced STEAM programs that add an *A* for the arts, principals can easily be swamped without the support of the central administration.

Here is where the central administration can be of great service to the principals in the district. They must ensure that adequate personnel are available in the schools to assist principals and teachers in implementing the approved program of studies. In addition, they should provide for the annual review of curriculum documents and the accompanying instructional materials. The reviews should be conducted by a committee of the appropriate teaching staff and include a review of the literature and invitations to external curriculum experts from nearby colleges and universities.

PEDAGOGY

Pedagogy is the art, science, or profession of teaching, or, more broadly, the theory and practice of education and its influences on the growth of learners. Pedagogy, taken as an academic discipline, is the study of how knowledge and skills are exchanged in an educational context, and it considers the interactions that take place during learning.

Theories of instruction long ago proposed by Jerome Bruner in his 1966 publication entitled *Toward a Theory of Instruction* have left generations of educators rich theoretical approaches to effective teaching and learning. One of the most well-known theories is that of modes of representation. It is a concept that has informed instructional practices related to mathematics education known as Bruner's model of Concrete-Representation-Abstract (CRA). It remains the practice of mathematics instruction advocated by the Singapore Ministry of Education since the early 1980s.[3]

Bruner's work, if even learned, is most likely forgotten after formal teacher training. Principals need to ensure that teachers are steeped in sound learning theories that inform and shape their practice. Here is where the central office can play a major role in providing in-service programs that highlight contemporary learning theories that can be easily applied to creating effective methods and materials for teachers at every level of instruction.

They need not be overly complex theories. Cognitive psychologist have long found that the most effective teaching approach to introducing a new or novel concept is to first begin by providing concrete experiences, then moving to more representative expression of the concept, and, finally, expressing the concept in abstract terms. For example, primary teachers will begin by teaching the concept of numbers by using a variety of concrete materials, for instance, Cuisenaire rods, then representing tally marks on a number line, and, lastly, introducing the 10 numerals (0–9) that make up our number system.

Unfortunately, at the secondary level, too few mathematics teachers' teachers are familiar with this learning theory and are quick to move to presenting abstract formulas rather than introducing concrete activities. For example, when introducing the formula for finding the area of a circle and the need to employ the pi ratio, teachers steeped in sound learning theories will have students select circular objects found in the room, provide them with string, and direct them to find the center of the circle (the diameter). Once they have found the diameter, they should be asked to find how many times the diameter will go around the outer rim of the circle (the circumference). After several tries, regardless of the size of the circle, they will discover the length of the diameter approximately three and one-seventh times (3.14) to cover the circumference. That ratio is what we call pi.

Not all theories fit as nicely into teaching as those pertaining to mathematics. Writing is one that comes to mind. It is illusive at best for most teachers regardless of the age of the students they teach. Nevertheless, there are a number of literacy theories that, if understood by teachers, can result in much-improved student writing. Few teachers are familiar with theories of language acquisition as proposed by psycholinguists. One that immediately comes to mind is Steven Pinker in his classic book *The Language Instinct*.[4] Pinker provides clear and concise writing as to how children acquire language and move on to be able to read and write—to be literate. A student of Norman Chomsky, he cites Chomsky's theories throughout the book, especially his notion of a universal grammar. Here, too, most teachers have only a superficial knowledge and understanding of these theories and the linguist responsible for them.

However, it does not mean that teachers with some training can begin to incorporate these theories so they become the basis for their instruction. The focus of the teaching of writing is too often on the grammatical rules and regulations, along with the need to include proper mechanics and punctuation. Such instruction represents the surface features of the writing, rather than the deeper rhetorical aspects. A simple theory that can easily be applied and captures what linguists refer to as deep rhetorical structures is to introduce students to the use of the rhetorical triangle—the writer, the context (subject or topic), and the audience.

The point of these illustrations is to encourage principals to work closely with their central office instructional support staff to provide teachers with an understanding of learning theories that can be the basis for building effective instruction. By no means should it be a task that is carried out by the principal. On the contrary, principals don't have the time to be aware of contemporary learning theories, nor should they be; however, they should insist that instructional supervisors or the assistant superintendent for curriculum and instruction, most likely located in their central office, provide ongoing pedagogical training to every teacher.

HIGH SCHOOL GRADUATES

In a recent report entitled "How the Other Half Learns: Reorienting an Educational System That Fails Most Students," Oren Cass, a senior fellow at the Manhattan Institute, claims our public education system is primarily designed to produce college graduates. He supports his contention by illustrating the fate of two high school graduates, one of whom he describes as having a "strong academic talent," while the other does not. One student receives extensive support in selecting a college or university and will most likely receive a four-year degree. The other is not likely to engage in any postsecondary schooling and, if the student does so, will probably not earn a degree.

Those who graduate and fail to complete even two years at a community college are regarded as failures. Cass points out that most Americans fit this profile and represent the working class. The report should be alarming to principals, superintendents, and boards of education. The key findings are as follows:

- Fewer than one in five high school graduates navigate easily through college and receive their degree in four years.
- A college degree does not guarantee entry into the middle class.
- Those with only a high school diploma can earn significantly more than many college graduates.
- The federal government spent only $1 billion on career and technical education (CTE) in 2016, while spending more than $70 billion in support of college attendance, a disparity that is also reflected at the state level.
- The educational reforms that have stressed high stakes standardized testing designed to improve academic achievement were poorly suited for those on the noncollege track.[5]

Cass makes a strong argument that students on the noncollege track deserve the same support as those students pursuing a college degree. Principals occupy a strategic position and, along with support from their superintendents and central office colleagues, can promote and bring about increased support for those seeking a technical career. Most comprehensive high schools have been slowly abolishing programs that could enhance students' chances of entering a technical field and have come to rely on vocational technical high schools, if available, in their districts.

Such comprehensive high schools do a disservice to those students who have no interest in entering a four-year college upon graduation. Principals must insist that school counselors be aware of these students early on and provide them, along with their parents, options other than four-year colleges or universities, while working to remove any socially constructed stigma.

Principals, with the support of their central office, can provide the district with information on their high school graduates beyond the typical report on where and what percentage of the graduates entered community colleges, technical schools, four-year colleges, military service, and the labor market.

Why not provide a means to follow up on the educational and career trajectories of their graduates? Such information is sure to be valued by students, teachers, the superintendent, and the board of education. After all, knowing what happens to our high school graduates is a good measure of the quality of education they received.

Why not, given today's technology, ask graduates to voluntarily fill out a form with their e-mail address to periodically track their postsecondary experiences? Many high school counselors stay in touch with former students for a short time, but that contact is far removed from any systematic tracking that could provide rich data on the lives of graduates. Tracking such data is much better than waiting to see who shows up at the annual class reunion.

SCHOOL LEADERSHIP TEAM

It is essential for principals to nurture positive and open relationships with their colleagues assigned to central office positions. Each will benefit from frequent planned interactions that occur both on and off the school grounds. Their colleagues in the central office can be a great resource for principals and should be included as part of the school's leadership team. When these relationships flourish, principals and the schools they lead are sure to thrive.

NOTES

1. Meredith I. Honig et al., *Central Office Transformation for District-Wide Teaching and Learning Improvement* (Seattle, WA: Center for the Study of Teaching and Policy, University of Washington, 2010), https://www.wallacefoundation.org/knowledge-center/Documents/Central-Office-Transformation-District-Wide-Teaching-and-Learning.pdf.

2. John Fitzsimons, "Connecting Our Staff to Their Professional Affiliations," *School Administrator* 69, no. 6 (2012): 16–17.

3. Leong Yew Hoog, Ho Weng, and Chen Lu Pien, "Concrete-Pictorial-Abstract: Surveying Its Origin and Charting Its Future," *Mathematics Educator* 16, no. 1 (2015): 1–19.

4. Steven Pinker, *The Language Instinct: How the Mind Creates Language* (New York: William Morrow and Company, 1994).

5. Oren Cass, "How the Other Half Learns: Reorienting an Educational System That Fails Most Students," *Manhattan Institute*, August 28, 2018, https://www.manhattan-institute.org/html/how-other-half-learns-reorienting-education-system-fails-most-students-11419.html.

FOUR
Thriving

Crucial Tasks and Effective Practices

> The goal of education is to enable individuals to continue their education. —John Dewey

Most superintendents, along with members of the central administration, often fail to provide strong support for both new and experienced principals. For far too long, principals have been left to flounder when they enter the principalship, receiving little more than a brief orientation to the school and their new office. The assumption is that principals possess the intellectual and emotional attributes necessary to be effective school leaders. After years of reflection and feedback from experienced principals, a list of crucial skills and practices that are essential to be an effective principal has emerged. They are skills and practices that principals need to hone with strong support from the superintendents and central office administrators.

The key skills and practices principals must master include planning, time management, fiscal allocations and building operations, leadership, and supervision and evaluation of personnel. In addition, effective principals may seek to incorporate the following operations and practices into their schools: increasing instructional time, scheduling only one lunch period, implementing a later school start time to combat sleep deprivation in adolescents, abolishing substitute teachers, and building political capital in support of changing the status quo.

PLANNING

The school day moves quickly, and principals get caught up in the whirlwind of activities. When they first arrive, they are given the keys to the office and a couple of memory sticks and are expected to forge ahead without little guidance. Principals soon learn that the position requires careful planning for the day, the week, and the year.

Given the technology of the 21st century, even those classified as digital immigrants (anyone born after the invention of the microchip) can learn to synchronize their calendars and share them with key staff. Principals, along with their assistant principals and administrative assistants, need to begin each week by planning ahead. Meeting with staff weekly will ensure a coordinated effort and clear distribution of assignments and work functions.

TIME MANAGEMENT

Time management, an essential skill, is often talked about but rarely thoroughly examined. We often hear the phrase, "My door is always open." The use of this phrase suggests that principals should always be accessible. Wrong! It violates an essential principle of good time management. Principals must be in control of their time—not others.

When their door is always open, they are no longer in control of their time. Others will see it as an open invitation to drop in and interrupt their work. A closed door prevents the drop-ins that are sure to occur when it is open. Save the office work for before and after school hours to cut down on disruptions and ensure that paperwork is accurate and coherent.

For principals to be viewed as friendly and accessible, they need to get out of the office and into the school while it is in session. They need to make frequent visits to the classrooms. Not a day should go by without the principal spending some time interacting with students and staff, and observing instruction.

In addition to visiting classrooms and remaining visible in the school, principals will be well served if they set aside time every few months to meet with the union leadership. Maintaining regular meetings with them provides a good opportunity to hear any labor or contractual issues that may be of concern. Being proactive, rather than waiting for a crisis to occur, will be in everyone's interests. Friendly relations where genuine concerns are discussed will most likely result in establishing good lines of communication and a healthy climate and morale among the members.

One other group principals must meet with on a regular basis is the school's parent organization. Maintaining a good working relationship with parents is a must. The primary function of the Parent–Teacher Association (PTA) is to be supportive of the school, as well as serve as a forum for the principal and the staff to engage the parents on all matters pertaining to curriculum and instruction at the school. It is an excellent arena in which to gain parent input on new initiatives or programs contemplated at the school.

Parents may also have an opportunity to express issues or concerns they may have, for instance, school security, extracurricular activities, or the need for additional resources. Principals and the schools are well served by maintaining an activate and vibrant parent–teacher association at the school. Such an association can be a rich resource, and those involved can be visible advocates for their child's school, as well as convey the importance of supporting quality educational in their community.

Secondary school parent groups are usually not as active as those in the middle school or elementary school. As the children enter their teen years, they seek more and more independence from their parents, and the parents, in turn, begin to distance themselves from the school. Nevertheless, a well-organized parent association is one the principals should encourage and promote.

RESOLVING PERSONNEL COMPLAINTS

One cautionary note: A PTA meeting is not the place to consider complaints about teachers and staff. Personnel issues are out of bounds in that forum. Complaints about teachers and staff are best resolved by following the district's complaint policy. Most policies follow a progressive format.

The first level encourages parents to communicate directly with the teacher; the second level requires the attention of the principal or designee; and the third involves district-level leadership. If a parent has a complaint that reaches the second phase and requires the attention of the principal, it is essential that the principal respond in a manner that is likely to create a greater degree of communication and enrich the relationships among the participants.

Principals must stress to parents or anyone who has an issue or complaint that they must follow the complaint policy; however, what is often left unsaid in the policy and must be reinforced is that when no satisfactory resolution has been reached at the first level meeting, the aggrieved party must inform the person or persons involved that they intend to move to the next level, which calls for informing the person's immediate supervisor.

Too often, especially in the case of a parent who brings the complaint to the attention of the teacher at the level-one meeting, then leaves the meeting without informing the teacher they are not satisfied with their response and plans to call their supervisor (in most cases, the principal). If the teacher is made aware of the parent's dissatisfaction with the initial meeting, they might be willing to work harder to resolve the complaint and not involve their immediate supervisor. Teachers feel circumvented when this occurs, and emotions are sure to rise.

When moved to level two, the principal's role in the meeting is to serve as a facilitator and be sure parent and teacher each have an opportunity to be heard. In some situations, it may be appropriate to have the school counselor be part of the meeting. To maintain a level of impartiality at the start of the process, the principal must avoid discussing the issue in advance of the meeting with either the teacher or parent. In the principal's first years, these meetings can quickly become difficult to manage. It is best to follow a well-established mediation protocol or practice like those recommended by Marshall Rosenberg's nonviolent communication method.[1]

Unfortunately, some faculty may believe it is the principal's role to "fix" personal problems they may be having with a colleague. Rather than address the issue directly with their colleague, they complain to the principal and ask that he or she intervene on their behalf. They are generally uncomfortable with directly addressing the problem with their colleague and wish to remain anonymous. Principals must never agree to intervene in this manner unless it involves a serious charge of possible unethical or criminal behavior that requires an immediate investigation and is clearly their responsibility to address.

The personnel conflicts that often arise are usually minor ones involving personality traits that can become an irritant. Examples might include the teacher who dominates the conversation, the neighboring teacher with a loud voice that can be heard down the hallway, the teacher who is always late to meetings, the teacher who rarely contributes ideas and suggestions, and the teacher who never shares ideas but is quick to adopt others initiatives and claim them as their own. These types of complaints are often brought to the principal's attention. Principals must advise their teachers that if such behavior is so troubling, they have an obligation to address the person directly as diplomatically as possible.

If relationships are valued among and between colleagues, problematic behaviors need to be addressed before too much harm occurs. If, on the other hand, it is a behavior that rises to a simple irritant and can be tolerated, it is best to be ignored. The principal should coach personnel at every level to resolve their issues with colleagues directly. If necessary, coach them by role-playing how to confront the problem without damaging the relationship.

Most of the personnel conflicts will not reach the level of the principal if teachers are provided with quality conflict resolution training. If left unresolved, provisions are usually made for a committee of board members to meet with the aggrieved parties—the last step in the process. Unfortunately, in some situations, the complaint goes beyond the bounds of the school policy and can be one where a legal suit is undertaken.

SETTING BOUNDARIES

It is essential for principals to set boundaries. They can be too accessible, to the detriment of their health and personal relationships. They need to manage just how accessible they are, especially with regard to text messages, voicemails, and e-mails. The downside to technology is that it makes one accessible 24/7. Superintendents should remind their principals to go home and shut off technology but be available to key personnel in case of a crisis.

FISCAL ALLOCATIONS AND BUILDING OPERATIONS

Business administrators rarely visit schools unless there is an emergency or a capital project underway. Most principals receive only a brief orientation about the construction of the school budget. That is not sufficient to grant a thorough understanding of the expenditures, revenues, and allocation of resources. The business manager should provide principals with one-on-one, scheduled on-site meetings to review every aspect of the school and district's budget. In addition, scheduled meetings of the head custodian, the director of buildings and grounds, the business manager, and the principal should take place throughout the year, for the purpose of touring the building and school grounds, and addressing any issues and possible needs for capital improvements.

LEADERSHIP

A graduate course in theories of leadership may provide a theoretical base for how one is to behave effectively; however, putting theory into practice requires much training and reflection. Principals could benefit greatly if provided with such training. As a practitioner, they need to "walk the talk." Here is an area where principals have to be aware of their leadership style and adjust it when situations call for it.

Superintendents can help by ensuring that the topic of effective leadership is part of every agenda. For example, reviews of contemporary leadership theories and how they can be applied to one's practice are a worthy topic of discussion. When appropriate, invite academics with expertise in effective leadership to address the district administrators.

SUPERVISION AND EVALUATION OF PERSONNEL

One of the most important tasks principals perform is the evaluation of personnel. It cannot take place once a year or every three years, as is often the case with tenured teachers. Unfortunately, with the advent of new personnel-evaluation approaches and the emphasis on value-added models based on standardized tests now in place in most states, principals are now required to evaluate teachers in such demeaning terms as "highly effective," "effective," "partially effective," and "ineffective." As many principals have found, this evaluation approach has created fear and uncertainty in teachers and does little to improve instruction. Regardless of what method the state requires, frequent positive and constructive interaction between principals and teachers remains essential and should be practiced and promoted by the superintendent.

The superintendent and central office team, oftentimes an untapped resource for principals, must provide effective instructional coaching no matter what evaluation plans a district implements. Coaching must take place in the schools, be ongoing, and incorporate frequent classroom walkthroughs with colleagues from the central office. In recognition of the complexity of the evaluation of personnel and the importance of supporting school principals in that process, many districts have employed trained coaches to work alongside their school principals. If a district does not provide such support, principals, along with colleagues, should press the district to employ professional coaches.

Principals may find their request fails to be heard. If so, they can resubmit the request with research on effective evaluation methods. Furthermore, cite the districts that have adopted the methods designed to improve instruction and promoted by the Wallace Foundation.[2]

INORDINATE SUPERVISORY RATIOS

In light of the pressure to hold teachers accountable, principals have been asked to exercise their formal authority to document and evaluate teachers, primarily through classroom observations. Only in schools does one find impossible ratios in which a supervisor is assigned from 30 to 50 people to supervise. Given that many teachers to supervise, principals are capable of conducting only two or three classroom observations during the course of a school year, and feedback is often delayed and infrequent. The traditional evaluation processes will have limited effects on changing behavior, especially when principals fall back on their positional power rather than develop supportive professional relationships.

It would be better if principals were to rely on two other sources of power that are more effective than positional power or the power of the office. Being a source of knowledge and resourceful while having an open and pleasing personality are the powers best relied on to be an effective leader. Principals who can exhibit all three powers are sure to be more successful in helping floundering new teachers, as well as ineffective experienced teachers.

Evaluation practices in most states now require the use of a four-point rating scale mentioned earlier. In addition, the evaluation includes a value-added component. Tied to the teacher's level of effectiveness is their students' performance, as measured by standardized tests. These evaluation systems have been found to be highly ineffective and have led to high rates of teacher turnover. They often result in superficial changes in behavior and reluctant compliance with those in authority.[3]

The new evaluation system put in place by the Obama administration through the Every Student Succeeds Act (ESSA) has increased principals' attention to and awareness of classroom instruction; however, the new system has created a major time management problem for principals. The evaluation process now requires extensive amounts of time to complete. It includes the following components:

- a self-evaluation submitted by the teacher
- a preconference meeting with the teacher
- a classroom observation session
- a written document in compliance with an established rubric
- a feedback conference with the teacher
- a student growth score based on a performance rubric

Thus, a substantive evaluation takes between 11 and 15 hours to complete.[4]

Principals cannot provide effective supervision given the number of teachers they are responsible for supervising. The large supervisory ratios that public-school principals encounter would never be found in private-sector workplaces. When added to the emphasis placed on the academic performance of students, based on their state standardized test scores, inordinate supervisory ratios create an environment designed to prevent the effective evaluation and supervision of staff.

Of course, the organizational structures found in schools vary. For example, some districts have district-wide supervisors who support the school principals, but they are rarely as effective as those supervisors housed in the schools. District supervisors are usually spread too thin to influence classroom instruction effectively. They serve the needs of the central office and the superintendent more often than those of the school principals.

In large high schools, there may be in place house structures in which a house master serves as the principal of each house and reports to the head master, who has oversight of the entire school. That organizational structure is generally better than one featuring district supervisors. It has been a long-standing tradition in many communities and is a good example of distributive leadership.

SUPPORT FOR STRUGGLING TEACHERS

What is most disturbing is that school systems provide little support to those teachers ill equipped to address the social and emotional issues that surface in their classrooms. Principals, along with their assistant principals, department chairs, school counselors, social workers, and school psychologists, are fully aware of those teachers who lack the intrapersonal skills to provide a supportive and respectful classroom environment. That, in turn, raises some questions. Are the principal and the support staff equipped to build a greater capacity in those struggling teachers to embody a healthier social and emotional learning environment? Can they effectively intervene if they themselves are not knowledgeable and understanding of social/emotional learning (SEL) and mindfulness interventions?

It is easy to identify those teachers who are struggling, but it is more challenging to provide appropriate support to them. Principals who wish to test that claim need only ask their administrators and pupil personnel staff to write down the names of struggling teachers—teachers who have limited tolerance for any misbehavior, rely on formal authority, exercise control with detentions, and have high rates of failures and referrals. With few exceptions, they will list the same teachers.

Now that everyone agrees who those struggling teachers are, what can be done to help them? If the administration and support staff want others to embody a healthy social and emotional learning environment, they themselves must first become fully engaged and knowledgeable in SEL practices and model them when appropriate.

PUPIL PERSONNEL STAFF

Knowing that there is little likelihood of principals receiving much support in the coaching and evaluation of teachers, why not turn to the pupil personnel staff (PPS) for help, while also pressing for the addition of coaches? School counselors, psychologists, and social workers have appropriate counseling and training skills in many areas that are sure to be lacking in struggling teachers. PPS members can support principals in providing appropriate interventions that may improve a teacher's instruction and interactions with students.

If necessary, is it not worth renegotiating their contracts to make such interventions part of the scope and responsibility of their positions? When asked to help their colleagues, most PPS members feel that their skills are being respected and valued. Any such staff member is likely capable of conducting a class meeting with a struggling teacher present. The goal of the classroom meeting is to address the issues that have interfered with maintaining a classroom environment conducive to positive teaching and learning. The opportunity for the teacher to observe a skilled group facilitator conducting the class meeting is a powerful but rarely used intervention. The PPS are capable of such interventions but, without additional support, can easily burn out. Without the principal's efforts to provide the needed support, the PPS may not be able to conduct the number of interventions needed to help their struggling colleagues.

Adding more responsibilities to a group that is stretched to the limits is not the answer unless additional personnel are added to support the PPS department. Here is where the principal has a strong argument for the need for more PPS or SEL coaches. After all, teachers are the most valuable and costly resource for the district. That said, why not do everything possible to ensure their continued success and improvement?

A principal's first course of action with regard to a struggling teacher should be to facilitate interventions designed to support that teacher. Infrequent classroom observations and evaluations that offer little feedback do little to improve the quality of instruction, while greatly demeaning the work of teachers.

To support everyone in the school community, why not employ the services of trained SEL coaches or additional members of the school mental health staff, for instance, school social workers? Both should have formal training in mental health strategies, including mindfulness-based interventions, counseling skills, and professional development skills that could help struggling educators.

Regardless of whether they hire SEL coaches or reimagine how support staff serves school communities, principals need to make the effort to challenge the traditional mindset and status quo. To build a truly collegial community of professionals who are willing to support one another and do what is best for their students, principals will need additional support. They are not likely to succeed without adding SEL personnel and doing everything they can to provide reasonable caseloads to their existing PPS. As difficult as it is, principals, especially those in underserved communities, must strive to have sufficient personnel assigned to their schools to lower class sizes and effectively address the needs of their teachers and students.

School budgets are a reflection of what is valued most. For too long, class sizes have been far too large, placing unacceptable demands on teachers at every level. PPS have been inadequately staffed and stretched to the point of limited effectiveness. It is not uncommon for elementary teachers to have more than 30 children in a class and for secondary teachers to have instructional responsibility for more than 125 students. In addition, school counselors are often responsible for more than 300 students, and school psychologists and social workers are often assigned to cover multiple schools in the district.

Principals witness the challenge to serve struggling teachers adequately every day while school is in session. It is time to take a stand and insist that the ratio of students to teachers and support staff be a reasonable one.

ASSISTANT PRINCIPALS

Assistant principals (APs), be they in elementary or secondary schools, typically have little responsibility for improving the quality of instruction, and that is most unfortunate. The traditional and most common role of the AP is to support the principal in the general administration of the school rather than serve as an instructional leader. They usually devote their time to such tasks as scheduling, budgeting, maintaining safety and security, and supervising noninstructional staff, and they often serve as the school disciplinarian. They may also be assigned to supervise teachers in large elementary schools; however, in most secondary schools, the supervision of teachers usually falls to the department chairs, if they have the appropriate certifications.

Ideally, the AP should function in all of the responsibilities required of the school principal. The principal should serve as the AP's mentor and ultimately be able to share the functions of administering the school with the AP. The AP position should be one designed to attract those who have the ambition for and interest in a career path that leads to the principalship. Some would argue that the roles are different, that not everyone is fit to be a principal, and that some APs should remain APs. That relationship should be the exception, but unfortunately, one will find it in place in too many schools.

The position should be understood to be one that is intended for those having the skill sets and the desire to be principals. With such an understanding and the expectations that accompany the role and responsibilities of the AP, the principal and the school community are more likely to be better served. Many in the position are skilled and comfortable in serving in the traditional AP role and, with some in-service training provided by the principal, can be effective instructional leaders, as well as administrative assistants.

DEPARTMENT CHAIRS

Much like APs, department chairs often have little to do with improving the quality of instruction, especially when a department chair is not in possession of a supervisory certificate. In most states, a department chair must hold a supervisory certificate to serve as a teacher's immediate supervisor. Otherwise, they function primarily as support staff to the members of the department and perform such roles as assisting the principal in the selection of teachers, mentoring new teachers, scheduling class assignments, budgeting, reviewing and implementing the curriculum, and purchasing instructional materials.

Traditionally, department chairs teach three to four classes and are given some release time from teaching to carry out their administrative functions. Many are natural and effective teacher coaches and excellent role models, especially for nontenured faculty; however, if left to serve in the more traditional role, they have little time for or impact on improving the quality of instruction.

An essential prerequisite to serve as a department chair is to be steeped in the knowledge of a particular discipline and the curriculum to which it adheres. In addition, department chairs must to be trained as skilled instructional supervisors and infused with an understanding of SEL practices. None of that will occur without the leadership of the school principal. It is the principal's responsibility to ensure all department chairs, along with their teachers, are trained and effectively implement social and emotional learning practices within their respective departments. Principals should do everything they can to provide their department chairs with adequate training and the formal authority to supervise the teachers in their departments.

Principals need to break with the status quo and have department chairs serve as both effective instructional leaders and formal supervisors. The role of the department chair needs to be transparent and understood by every teacher in the department. For too long, there has existed a quasi-supervisory relationship between department chairs and teachers. It has often led to fractionalized relationships within departments and between the chairs and the principals, especially when a teacher in a chair's department is failing to perform effectively.

PROBATIONARY PERIOD

In most states newly hired teachers are given a three-year probationary period to establish tenure in their position. There are exceptions; California offers a two-year probationary period. If performance is judged as satisfactory, their contract is renewed. It is a crucial period and one that is often neglected because of inadequate supervisory staff that results in too few classroom observations.

Some districts, in addition to the traditional classroom observations, require the probationary teachers to submit videotapes of their teaching: One teacher selected a tape that is an example of effective instruction in the first several months and one final tape at the close of the school year. The tapes are used as part of a total evaluation system. They are viewed by a juried and trained group of supervisors based on a teaching rubric developed by the district. The supervisory group includes the principal and or the immediate supervisor.

In an October 11, 2018 article in *Education Week* by Madeline Will, she cites six evaluation systems that have been judged effective by the National Council on Teacher Quality (NCTQ). NCTQ found that these systems contain the following attributes, which result in an effective evaluation system: multiple measures for rating a teacher, including classroom observations, student surveys, and measures of student achievement; at least three rating categories; annual observations and evaluations for teachers; written feedback after each observation; and professional development and compensation tied to evaluations.

REMOVAL OF INEFFECTIVE TEACHERS

Despite a principal's best efforts to provide coaching and support in the most respectful and caring manner possible, ineffective teachers may at times fail to improve. In such cases, principals have little recourse other than to notify the teachers that they are at risk of losing their jobs. The first step is to meet with the teachers and attempt to counsel them by pointing out that some people are just not a good fit for teaching. They may have made a mistake in choosing teaching as a career. If the teachers are willing, why not, if possible, offer career counseling sessions aimed at finding them a more suitable career? The district would pay for the career counseling sessions.

These conversations are stressful but cannot be avoided, no matter how difficult the personal circumstances of the teacher in question. To avoid conflict with a teacher's union, a principal will need to document the number of interventions and forms of support provided to the struggling teacher. The approach with regard to the union should be to seek their help, advice, and cooperation before any formal process to terminate the teacher's employment begins. By all means, principals should avoid engaging in adversarial exchanges with union leadership.

When principals are moved to recommend the dismissal of a tenured teacher, they must be prepared for a lengthy and time-consuming process of collecting reams of evidence that supports their recommendation. Sadly, it is a process that rarely results in the termination of a tenured teacher. A principal is more likely to elicit a resignation if supported by the teacher's union and in possession of documented evidence that the teacher has received sufficient support to improve his or her performance. It is understood that no principal or union leader wishes to end a teacher's employment or livelihood. Nonetheless, those involved must keep in mind that ensuring the welfare of the students is their primary responsibility.

INCREASING INSTRUCTIONAL TIME

The research remains inconclusive on how the length of the school year and the school day affect overall student performance. One of the most frequently cited measures of student performance is the Program for International Student Assessment (PISA). Administered by the Organization for Economic Cooperation and Development (OECD), PISA examinations in 2015 included 540,000 15-year-olds representing 72 nations, one of which was the United States. The exams tested the mathematics, science, and reading performance of the students.

Finland, although it has a shorter school year and less emphasis on standardized tests and homework, consistently ranks among the highest-performing countries as measured by PISA. The United States performed poorly in 2015, scoring in the middle of the global pack behind many other advanced industrialized nations. The United States ranked 19th in science, 20th in reading, and 31st in mathematics out of the 35 OECD countries in the 2015 tests.

Most principals, if they could, would like to see the amount of classroom instruction increase. The belief is that more time in class will result in improved performance; however, little has been done to increase instructional time. Many school districts have added days to the school year to provide in-service programs for the professional staff, which is costly and has had no effect on increasing instructional time. Yet, there are ways for principals, superintendents, and boards of education to increase classroom time without generating exorbitant costs, violating their labor contracts, or adding days to the school calendar.

While elementary teachers are usually given blocks of 60 or more minutes to devote to teaching literacy and numeracy skills, secondary teachers are allocated periods of between 40 and 45 minutes to teach specific subjects. The issues of how much time schools should allocate for instruction and how best to distribute the time across subject areas and grade levels remain very much alive and well.

Debates continue about whether the United States has too short a school year or school day compared to other countries. Calls for a longer school year and longer school day persist, especially among politicians. Governors, for example, are not shy about calling for a longer school day and longer school year. They and their supporters never examine how time is distributed in the traditional school day. The idea is usually dropped when the costs of adding days to the school year are calculated.

The issue of how time is distributed is most pronounced in secondary schools, in which the program of studies is divided into specific subjects. Secondary schools must comply with state educational requirements, along with the local district's discretion on elective subject offerings. As a result, the student scheduling process at secondary schools is more complicated. For example, most secondary schools maintain traditional fixed time slots for classes, the majority of which meet every day.

However, some high schools and middle schools have moved to block scheduling, in which class periods range from one hour to an hour and a half, rotate throughout the week, and do not meet every day. Secondary-school principals who operate with the traditional eight-period class schedule should consider changing to a rotating block schedule. They will find it significantly increases the length of an instructional period.

ROTATING BLOCK SCHEDULE

According to the National Center for Educational Statistics, the average length of a secondary-school day is 6.8 hours, or 408 minutes. If a 408-minute day includes 8 periods, a 40-minute lunch, and 4 minutes of passing time between classes, what remains for instruction is 340 minutes. Thus, in an eight-period day with only 340 minutes remaining, each class can be no longer than 42.5 minutes. Many secondary schools allow students to carry as many as nine classes per day. A nine-period day would allow only 37.7 minutes per class, entirely too little time to cover the prescribed curriculum.

But, with a six-period day schedule, including a 40-minute lunch period and four minutes to pass from class to class, what remains for instruction is 344 minutes. In a six-period day, the classes can be as long as 57.3 minutes. This includes dropping one class period per day and dropping from eight to seven periods, or one less subject for a student to carry. Revising the school schedule is one practical, inexpensive means of increasing instructional time. By having classes meet four out of five days per week, rather than every day, schools can enable instructional time to be increased from the typical 40 minutes per class to almost one hour.

One of the more popular schedules consists of six blocks (see appendixes F and G) of time, three in the morning and three in the afternoon. Each block can be as long as one hour if it meets four times per week, allowing the student to carry seven classes per week in what is referred to as a drop-rotating schedule. The rotation is usually conducted by rotating the three blocks before lunch and the three blocks after lunch, with one block dropping out in each rotation.

This strategy reduces the frequency of class meetings but significantly increases each class's instructional time. In addition to increasing instructional time, rotating the classes ensures that the first class meeting of the day is never fixed. That is particularly important in secondary schools with early start times, as the first class of the day usually has higher levels of student absenteeism and tardiness from sleep-deprived adolescents. Having a thousand or more students changing classes eight or nine times in a day can only be described as frenetic.

IMPROVING CONDITIONS FOR TEACHING AND LEARNING

Adding instructional time significantly improves teaching and learning conditions. First, the negative effects of student downtime are reduced. Research suggests that even the best-planned and most ideally managed classes have an average of three to four minutes of downtime before students are fully engaged in their lessons. Principals and supervisors have long observed that downtime further limits the kind of activities teachers can offer in a typical 40-minute class period.

Teachers feel pressured and frustrated with so little time and are forced to move quickly through the required curriculum or eliminate sections entirely. They have acknowledged that additional time enables them to better engage their students in various instructional activities, including role-playing, debates, problem solving, and simulations. The dominant mode of instruction when the time allocated per class is limited tends to be lecturing. There is nothing wrong with lecturing, but learning is best when learners have opportunities to be active participants in their learning.

Additional instructional time is particularly valuable to classes that traditionally require preparation. For example, most lab science classes are scheduled as a double period to conduct laboratory experiments, which require time to set up and break down equipment, as well as conduct the laboratory exercise. The same holds true for music and art classes, in which students are active in working with instruments or tools, be they paint brushes or potter's wheels.

More importantly, longer class periods give every teacher, regardless of subject, the opportunity to rely less on lecturing and engage the students in more active learning exercises. Additional instructional time frees them from relying on the traditional role of the "sage on the stage" and allows them to be more of a facilitator than a dispenser of information. Of course, more instructional time has little or no effect if not used wisely. The United States has a longer school day than many countries, but what is important is how the time is distributed. Moving frequently from class to class during the course of a nine-period day eats up time (three to four minutes with every change) and leaves too few minutes to allocate for classroom instruction.

In light of the benefits of increased instructional time, why do schools operate with as many as nine classes per day? Try shadowing a student carrying nine classes per day to see what it is like to be moving that frequently throughout the school. Most likely, those carrying that many classes are students who, along with their parents and school counselors, believe that doing so will improve their chances of being accepted to a highly competitive college or university. In some cases, they do not have time for a scheduled lunch and instead eat a yogurt or sandwich at their desk or lab station.

There is no evidence that the more courses a student takes, the better their chances of being accepted to a college or university. College admission officials state that the important factor is not how many courses a student has completed, but how well the student performed. Yes, some exceptional students perform very well while completing nine classes per day, but such a stressful schedule can prevent them from experiencing the pleasures of learning, as well getting adequate sleep. It is a cruel practice, and principals should do everything they can to ensure that it is not carried out in their schools.

Principals may face contractual restrictions when seeking to alter the school schedule. For example, in New York City, the contractual day for a teacher is six hours and 20 minutes. Far too often, the school district's legal contract takes precedence over the obligation of educators to uphold their social contract. Promoting what is best for the welfare of the students sometimes remains in the shadows. Three other suggestions that should enhance the overall day-to-day operation at secondary schools are to establish one lunch period (the unit lunch), abolish the need for substitute teachers, and start the school day no earlier than 8:30 a.m.

THE UNIT LUNCH

Most large secondary schools have multiple lunch waves because of the limited seating capacity of their school cafeterias; however, many high schools have only one lunch period, even though their cafeteria cannot seat the entire school. Principals have worked with the school's dietician and kitchen staff to provide enough options to move the entire school through the cafeteria quickly and efficiently by setting up separate food stations. For example, a salad bar, a ready-made sandwich station, a hot meals bar, and a drinks-only bar, may be set up to provide easy access to students.

If the cafeteria cannot seat the entire school's population, where can students be seated? In many schools that have implemented a single lunch period, students are allowed to eat in areas of the school other than the lunchroom. Schools have allowed students to eat in designated classrooms, locker alcoves, classrooms with their club advisors, and, weather permitting, outside patio areas with lunch tables and chairs. Many schools have open-campus policies that allow students to leave the school grounds for lunch.

Another benefit of having one lunch period for students, faculty, and administrators is that it allows ample opportunities for students to meet with teachers, counselors, club advisers, and PPS staff. The PPS can either have a luncheon meeting with the students or choose to eat at a later time, since they are not assigned to teach classes. In some districts, club activities are scheduled to meet during the unit lunch period. Clubs no longer have to be scheduled after school hours and compete with the school's interscholastic athletic programs or other extracurricular activities.

Principals seeking to implement the unit lunch need to be ready for pushback from their custodial staff, who will be understandably concerned with the cleanliness of the building, especially litter problems. Some parents will also be opposed to an open-campus policy, allowing students to leave the school for lunch.

Each of these hurdles can be easily resolved. Ample wastebaskets can be placed in strategic locations. Students enjoy the freedom that comes with the unit lunch options and will work to police areas to ensure they are free of litter. They understand that if they do not, they risk losing the unit lunch schedule. Lastly, schools may implement a policy in which no student may leave the school grounds for lunch without retaining written permission from their parents. Usually, only upperclassmen are given the option to leave the school grounds for lunch.

COMBATTING SLEEP DEPRIVATION

If principals and superintendents would take the time to review the literature and the importance of sufficient sleep for adolescents, they would find substantial support and reasons to change to later school starting and ending times. Perhaps most notable is the inextricable link between sleep and learning. The Center for Sleep and Wake Disorders has found that without adequate sleep, adolescents process information differently, which, in turn, has a negative effect on school performance. A 2012 study published in *Child Development* similarly found that when adolescent students sleep less to study more, they have trouble comprehending class material and struggle with assignments and tests the following day.[5]

Although the National Sleep Foundation has determined that American teenagers require about nine and one-quarter hours of sleep a night, a study published in the *Journal of Adolescent Health* found that two-thirds of high school students sleep for no more than seven hours each night.[6] That lack of sleep potentially harms physical growth and brain development by lowering the level of human growth hormone the adolescents' bodies produce. Studies have also linked a lack of sufficient sleep to depression and warned that energy drinks containing high concentrations of caffeine, which many teens consume to stay awake, could harm adolescents' neurological and cardiovascular systems.

Despite the wealth of research on sleep deprivation and its detrimental effects on adolescents, most high schools throughout the United States begin the day before 8:00 a.m. and end before 3:00 p.m. Added to the early start is the length of the bus ride, which can vary from less than 20 minutes to one hour, depending on a student's proximity to the school. The problem is more apparent in suburban and rural school districts serving large townships and counties.

Principals need not be discouraged when they encounter the ever-present organizational resistance to change. Resistance comes from many quarters. One loud voice opposing change frequently comes from a school's athletic department—a department that carries much political clout, as most principals know. Generally, coaches resist any change in scheduling, fearing that a late school dismissal time will wreak havoc on scheduling games and contests, especially "away games," which require long bus rides. Resistance also comes from working parents, teachers included, who are unwilling to adjust their personal schedules, as well as from students who have after-school jobs.

With such resistance, and so little political will on the part of educational leaders, one can see why early start and dismissal times remain firmly in place. Nevertheless, in light of the compelling research on sleep deprivation and its negative effects on adolescents, secondary-school principals must do everything they can to implement a later start time and overcome the resistance they are sure to encounter.

Parents are well aware that their young children go to bed much earlier and wake much earlier than their teenagers. Nevertheless, the early start time remains firmly in place and is accompanied by excessive tardiness in first-period classes. The failure of districts to address the issue of sleep deprivation is truly troubling. Secondary-school principals need to step up and insist that their districts recognize the negative consequences of early start times for adolescents. Those in leadership positions must work to educate parents and board of education members about the negative consequences of too little sleep.

NO SUBSTITUTE POLICY

When teachers are absent, most high schools hire substitutes to cover their classes. Asked to explain why, the administrative response is typically reflexive: "We've always hired substitutes." When it is pointed out to teachers that most substitutes have no formal training or in-depth understanding of the subjects they may be asked to teach, the response is often that every teacher is required to provide their substitutes with lesson plans. The practice of providing a substitute teacher for a short-term absence of a day or two from high school classes, not a long-term absence in which a qualified and certified substitute would be required, is a questionable practice and one that principals should eliminate.

With the exception of such planned absences as professional-development and personal days, teachers do not know when they will be absent from school. Principals need to take the time to examine substitute plans. They will find that such plans generally have little instructional value and are usually designed to keep students engaged and busy for the length of the class period. Most often, the plans include reading assignments or film viewings that may—or may not—be timely in terms of the scope and sequence of the curriculum.

Furthermore, hiring substitutes can be an administrative nightmare. Most school districts contract with substitute services. With few exceptions, these services experience frequent turnover. Often, first-time subs arrive late or not at all, and the members of the administrative staff scramble to find a free teacher to supervise the class. When no teacher is to be found, the principals or one of their assistants will have to cover the class.

Teacher-absenteeism rates are generally between 3 and 4 percent a year. Knowing that untrained subs will provide little instructional continuity for the students, why do schools hire them, and why do they incur an expense that may run in the tens of thousands of dollars? A school employing 100 teachers may surpass $100,000 in substitute pay each year. In sum, why should a practice that is of little or no instructional benefit, expensive, and an administrative nightmare be continued?

Generally, the justification is as follows: "Adolescents make poor choices and need to be closely supervised." Yet these are the same students who frequently babysit for neighbors and friends, and are left alone to supervise and protect children, homes, and valuable possessions. Is there a mixed message here?

Some may argue that teachers and administrators have a legal obligation to supervise students and risk being sued for gross negligence if they leave students unsupervised; however, students are housed in schools staffed with teachers, administrators, clerks, administrative assistants, custodians, and security personnel. The reality is that the adult-to-student ratio in most schools likely approaches or exceeds one adult to every 10 students. Does this reflect a lack of adequate supervision?

In districts that have implemented no-substitute policies (see appendix G), schools have taken a variety of steps to provide their students with options that they could exercise when a teacher is absent. For example, many teachers have organized their students into study groups that could meet in the cafeteria, library, or auditorium. Those locations were designated as supervised areas for students not in class. Some teachers arranged for students to audit other classes, work on art projects, practice music, or engage in club activities with the prior approval of the appropriate colleagues.

Allowing students opportunities to manage their time affords them a real understanding of the consequences of good and poor time management. Many students will continue their education beyond high school.

When a college instructor or professor is absent, it is highly unlikely that the college will provide a substitute teacher. Students can choose to go back to bed or go to the library to study. The decision is theirs to make.

For those students who directly enter the world of work or the armed forces, good time management is a prerequisite for success and required for continued employment. It is a responsibility that comes with growing up. What better time to begin learning this valuable skill than while in school? It may even reduce the college dropout rate.

Approximately 40 percent of students who enter college fail to graduate within six years.[7] Rather, they leave with no degree and staggering debt. Principals do a disservice to their high school students if they do not provide them with opportunities to make choices and learn to manage their time. Principals can begin by doing away with the practice of hiring short-term substitute teachers.

Some educators may also argue that they have no option other than to have students supervised by a substitute teacher. Nonetheless, if they shift the focus from a custodial function to learning opportunities, many viable options will emerge. Schools can offer better educational choices to their students than a substitute-led class. Principals and their faculty should provide students with sound educational options rather than allow them to be babysat by a substitute who knows little about the subject and even less about the students.

CHALLENGING THE STATUS QUO

Principals who decide to move in this direction will face several challenges. These challenges will surface any time something as significant as a change to the school's schedule or the elimination of substitute teachers is attempted. The first challenge is inertia. It is much easier to maintain the status quo than create unrest and uncertainty. Principals are sure to hear that annoying phrase, "If it ain't broke, don't fix it."

Begin by seeking support for such changes from the superintendent and fellow administrators, as well as faculty, student leaders, and PTA officers. Avoid the "hard sell" approach. Rather, listen carefully to any concerns or issues that surface, and provide ample information and relevant research. If possible, cite nearby districts that have instituted some of the proposed changes you are promoting. To avoid grudging compliance and resistance from teachers, parents, and school board members, principals should seek support from and build political capital with those who would be directly affected by any proposed change in school operations.

Once a principal has gathered sufficient support to explore such changes, a good strategy to use when challenging deeply imbedded practices is to form a problem-solving committee of faculty, students, and parents. Such a committee would do the following:

- Describe the proposed change.
- List the possible pros and cons.
- Provide opportunities for those affected to voice their concerns.
- Agree that any change should be evaluated within a reasonable period of time.
- Agree that no change be made without the approval of the committee by group consensus (avoid voting).
- Implement the change.
- Evaluate and, if necessary, refine the plan after several months of operation.
- Keep the board of education apprised from start to finish.

These steps, while time consuming, allow those directly affected by the proposed changes to become involved in and take ownership of the decision.

POLITICAL AWARENESS

A superintendent can serve as a great resource for a district's principals, helping them recognize and understand the political influence of the various powerbrokers in the community, how they impact the schools, and how to gain their support. Groups like a school's PTA, the local collective bargaining leaders and representatives, and the informal faculty leaders at each school hold the political capital. The principal must establish clear boundaries and good working relationships with each of them.

CELEBRATE AND SUPPORT

After conducting a thorough search and selecting the best candidate for the position of principal, a district's superintendent and administrators are foolish and derelict if they do not do everything they can to ensure the principal's success. The job description is exhaustive, and what is suggested here, although essential, does not encompass the total role and responsibilities of the school principal. A system's administrators must not only support their principals, but also periodically celebrate and acknowledge the principals' dedication, hard work, and value to the school district.[8]

NOTES

1. Marshall Rosenberg, *Living Nonviolent Communication: Practical Tools to Connect and Communicate Skillfully in Every Situation* (Boulder, CO: Sounds True, 2012).

2. Kenneth Leithwood et al., *How Leadership Influences Student Learning* (2004), https://www.wallacefoundation.org/knowledge-center/Documents/How-Leadership-Influences-Student-Learning.pdf.

3. Valerie Strauss, "What the Research Really Says on Teacher Evaluation," *Washington Post*, September 16, 2012, https://www.washingtonpost.com/blogs/answer-sheet/post/what-research-really-says-on-teacher-evaluation/2012/09/16/2e9de9fa-ff44-11e1-8adc-499661afe377_blog.html?utm_term=.bf5f42eb2835.
Richard Rothstein, "Teacher Accountability and the Chicago Teachers Strike," *Economic Policy Institute*, September 14, 2012, https://www.epi.org/blog/teacher-accountability-chicago-teachers.

4. Denisa Superville, "Teacher Evaluations Have Dramatically Changed the Principal's Job," *Education Week*, November 13, 2018, https://www.edweek.org/ew/articles/2018/11/14/teacher-evaluations-have-dramatically-changed-the-principals.html.

5. Cari Gillen-O'Neel et al., "To Study or to Sleep? The Academic Costs of Extra Studying at the Expense of Sleep," *Child Development* 84, no. 1 (August 2012): 133–42.

6. Danice K. Eaton et al., "Prevalence of Insufficient, Borderline, and Optimal Hours of Sleep Among High School Students—United States, 2007," *Journal of Adolescent Health* 46, no. 4 (April 2010): 399–401.

7. "Fast Facts," *National Center for Education Statistics*, https://nces.ed.gov/fastfacts/display.asp?id=40.

8. This chapter is based in part upon the following publications: John Fitzsimons, "First-Year Principals: What They Really Need to Know," *Principal Leadership* 17, no. 8 (April 2012): 52–55; John Fitzsimons, "You Snooze You Lose? Maybe Not," *School Leader* 44, no. 6 (May/June 2014): 10–11; John Fitzsimons, "Make Every Minute Count," *School Leader* 45, no. 1 (July/August 2014): 26–29; John Fitzsimons, "Adding Instructional Time at No Greater Cost," *School Administrator* 68, no. 10 (November 2011): 40–41; John Fitzsimons, "Don't Hire Substitute Teachers in High School," *Education Week* 32, no. 1 (April 21, 2012): 3.

FIVE
Building a Safe, Social, Emotional, and Academic School Environment

> You cannot teach today the same way you did yesterday to prepare students for tomorrow. —John Dewey

Educational reformers, intent on holding the public schools accountable to a set of common core standards and focused on academic achievement, have overlooked the foundational relationship between academic learning and social/emotional learning (SEL). All too often, SEL is seen as a soft add-on or a "nice touch" when, in fact, it is an essential building block of a quality school system.[1]

Individuals are composed of complex neurobiological mechanisms. Those mechanisms work through a double lens: first, to keep us alive, and second, to support our thriving. To put it simply, all must be well in the primitive aspects of our brains and bodies for more complex functions, for instance, academic learning, to be supported. If all is not well regulated, the system limits access to crucial learning centers in the prefrontal cortex, for example, until the crisis is over.[2]

Thus, it is essential for children to feel safe and supported in school. In addition, the neurobiological health and development of young children depends on well-regulated adult systems. In addition to the individual mechanisms at work within each of us, it is just as important to note that the intersecting social and cultural systems within the school community form the container in which well-regulated children can grow.[3] Furthermore, children who experience severe emotional and social suffering may become a grave danger to their communities. Of course, schools are not solely responsible for the mental health crisis in the United States, but when reformers and school leadership fail to recognize the importance of the social and emotional health of students and school communities, the consequences can be tragic, as has been the case in the all-too-frequent school shootings occurring throughout the nation. When principals attempt to maintain safe and secure schools by establishing and enforcing rules and regulations embedded in zero-tolerance policies, they fail to address the underlying causes and gain only temporary fixes.

SOCIAL AND EMOTIONAL LEARNING

The principal must lead, promote, and provide the social/emotional training of their teachers and students. To do so, they must become familiar with current research-based models of the effects of employing a social and emotional learning environment in schools. Pupil personnel directors, school social workers, counselors, and school psychologists must support their principals in establishing and maintaining a healthy social and emotional school climate. To enforce the shared responsibility for discipline, principals must insist that teachers join with them in responding to students who misbehave in the classroom. A positive student–teacher relationship is much more important than doling out consequences for misbehavior. It is the cornerstone of future positive behavioral outcomes.

Educators must recognize that if children are to progress academically, they require a socially and emotionally safe and secure environment in which to learn. The need for an emotionally safe and secure environment, although a widely understood and acceptable notion supported by decades of research, is often overlooked. Of course, to make systemic changes that support a more supportive/restorative school culture, resources must be allocated. Yet, even with limited resources, principals must encourage their teachers to engage in their own social/emotional growth, as well as integrate SEL into their classrooms. SEL programs should not take a back seat to cocurricular activities and athletic programs, no matter how limited the school resources.

The programs must be especially attuned to children with academic difficulties that readily surface in their struggles to gain literacy and numeracy skills encountered in the primary grades. As these students age through the system, they fall farther and farther behind despite being enrolled in academic intervention services (AIS). The interventions are usually delivered in small pullout groups, which tend to label students publicly and isolate them socially. Principals should insist that these students receive counseling services along with AIS. Often, the root cause of their academic problems rests in their underdeveloped social and emotional skills.

When young elementary students feel anxious or insecure, access to the neurobiological mechanisms in the brain are blocked. When that happens, children may not be able to express themselves appropriately; however, the signs are usually very apparent to teachers. The children may be quiet and isolated from their peers, frustrated and prone to striking out physically, or defiant. When inappropriate behavior occurs, some teachers are too quick to suspect a learning disability rather than consider the intrapersonal dynamics within the student, the social dynamics of the classroom, and other social contexts within which the child lives.

Here is where a trained staff member could provide support to the classroom teacher. Together, they could examine the social and emotional climate of the classroom before referring the child for an evaluation by the special education department. Attention to the classroom climate is mandated as part of the response to intervention (RTI); however, existing practices often fall short, as they fail to integrate SEL practices.

Here, too, principals need to voice strong support for adequate counseling services. Sadly, few elementary schools are staffed with school counselors, and many of the counselors are not trained in supporting entire classrooms in using effective SEL practices. School psychologists and social workers, often spread too thin over many schools, are limited in what they can offer to teachers and students. In addition, the psychologists, responding to the overwhelming number of special education referrals, function primarily as psychometricians, administering intelligence tests and evaluating students for possible learning disabilities.

To maintain a sound SEL environment, school principals must advocate for investing in training for all school personnel in evidence-based SEL practices, increasing mental health staff to reduce staff-to-student ratios, and focusing on a greater coordination between teachers and mental health staff.

SECONDARY-SCHOOL DROPOUTS

High school principals are no strangers to the problem of dropouts. There are many reasons for students to drop out, but there is one principals may prevent if they are sensitive to and aware of tensions in the school's climate. It occurs when secondary students feel unaccepted by their peers and disrespected by their teachers, and the school climate for them becomes toxic. When that happens, they simply drop out. Middle school principals report the usual patterns of behavior of disaffected students. They usually have terrible attendance, fail most of their subjects, frequently challenge authority, or withdraw from active participation or interest in after-school activities the school offers. Too young to drop out, they nevertheless have done so.

Secondary principals need to be ready to provide support to those students who enter secondary schools carrying heavy social and emotional baggage that has plagued their academic performance throughout their formal schooling. Why not help teachers be in touch with their own feelings by listening to and sensing what others are feeling? It is a good way for them to become more empathetic toward struggling students.

Principals need to recognize that a skilled and caring staff, along with a menu of appropriate interventions, is required to meet the social and emotional needs of these students. Otherwise, these underdeveloped students will rarely gain the proficiency levels required to graduate from high school. Principals sadly watch them drop out of school prematurely.

These students are too often placed in special education classes and identified as learning disabled, which further alienates them in the school. Regardless of the level of the school in which principals serve, they must recognize that for many of their students labeled as learning disabled, the problem rests in a dysfunctional educational system—not in the students. Is there something principals can do to develop the social and emotional skills of teachers and students?

MINDFULNESS RESEARCH

The quick-fix one- or two-day workshops on conflict-resolution skills or SEL offered during scheduled in-service days are rarely enough to bring about any sustained changes in current school practices. Given that education has always been in search of the "what works holy grail," why haven't great, well-researched, and validated approaches taken root? They come and then they go. The question of how to achieve enduring adaptation is one that has plagued educators. The latest promising approach is mindfulness training.

Yet, it has been around a long time. Jon Kabat-Zinn developed a Mindfulness-Based Stress Reduction Program (MBSRP) in 1979, housed in the Center for Mindfulness in Medicine, Health Care, and Society, at the University of Massachusetts Medical School. Kabat-Zinn defines mindfulness as "paying attention to the present moment, on purpose, and with a nonjudgmental attitude." The center's mission is to "explore, understand, articulate, and further mindfulness in the lives of individuals, organizations, and communities through clinical, rigorous scientific research, professional training, and informed public discourse."[4] Why not investigate the practice of mindfulness-based social emotional programs and practices?

In addition to the MBSRP programs, the University of Wisconsin's Center for Investigating Healthy Minds (CIHM) operates a laboratory dedicated to exploring mindfulness and mediation practices, and their effects on the physiology of the brain and behavior. They have accumulated decades of research that supports the practices of mindfulness and meditation. An increasing number of schools have promoted and cultivated a deepened awareness and insight through the practice of mindfulness and meditation. Through such practices, schools have increased the capacity for every child to learn, especially children who exhibit less control in regulating their behavior.[5]

CIHM studies have found that the practice of mindfulness results in physical, psychological, and social benefits. The center's researchers conducted a small study to test the effects of an eight-week mindfulness course designed for teachers. The results were promising. They found that teachers who completed the course reported such personal benefits as increased levels of compassion, decreased anxiety and depression, and less burnout. Moreover, the teachers' classroom-management skills and emotional and instructional support of students were judged more effective as a result of the mindfulness training.[6]

Granted, the practice of mindfulness in school settings is relatively new; however, interest in mindfulness is rapidly growing, given the evidence of its positive outcomes. Studies conducted both inside and outside of the classroom suggest that mindfulness training improves the overall well-being and success of participants. Researchers know more about how the brain functions than ever before. Is it not time for schools to use those new neurological findings to enhance teaching and learning for every student, regardless of personal history and readiness to learn?

The growing body of research on mindfulness in school-based contexts reveals the following list of core benefits:

- increased sense of calm
- better focus and concentration
- decreased stress and anxiety
- improved impulse control
- increased self-awareness
- more skillful responses to difficult emotions
- increased empathy and understanding[7]

Led by the school principal, the integration of mindfulness into the school setting will give educational reforms the foundation necessary for the other components to take hold and lead all teachers and students toward success. Questions remain: Will it take hold, or will it be just another passing fad? Will principals be motivated to acquire the skills and political will to move their schools in that direction, or will mindfulness go the way of other interventions and die on the vine?

INTEGRATION

The integration of the academic, social, and emotional aspects of school, along with mindfulness practices, might just be the right recipe for what is missing in today's educational reform movement. The shift toward what has been uncovered in the neurosciences may not yet be widely valued or understood by reform leaders. Here is where school principals, who occupy a crucial leadership position, can be instrumental in promoting the practices of mindfulness-based programs in their schools. Once reformers become familiar and comfortable with the approaches and techniques of mindfulness, will they understand why it is an essential element of a sound, secure, and healthy learning environment? Will those principals who serve children in poor rural and urban neighborhoods—children who come to school with many social, emotional, and economic disadvantages—see the benefits of integrating these practices into their schools?

RESTORATIVE JUSTICE

Regardless of the organizational structure of the school, staff members like assistant principals, department chairs, and housemasters must be essential players in helping principals maintain a safe and secure emotional environment. They, along with the faculty and staff, must be well trained in SEL and the principles and approaches found in restorative justice training, especially since they are often the first to be called on when there is a serious infraction by a student. If not sufficiently trained in those approaches, they can often exacerbate the situation. They are more likely to recommend in-school or out-of-school suspension, which has little impact on changing behavior.

Many schools, for example, the Oakland Unified School District, have implemented and expanded their restorative justice programs. Oakland Unified School District's program, which began in 2007, includes a three-tier approach. The first tier takes place in a school-wide community-building meeting, which serves as a space to voice issues and concerns, and promote and encourage peer-to-peer respect. The second tier addresses a specific infraction or conflict. Here the harmed students, along with those causing the harm, are brought together with their peers and adults to discuss and resolve the issue. The third tier is reserved for the reintegration of a student following a serious infraction that has resulted in a suspension.[8]

The restorative justice approach has been borrowed from various indigenous cultures and is based on the belief that people want to be part of a healthy community. The approach has resulted in reduced suspensions and improved school attendance. Its strength lies in the underlying principle that school discipline is the collective responsibility of the entire school community, not just the administration. The Oakland District now has an Office of Organizational Effectiveness, designed to promote and implement its core values, the first of which is to "provide multiple learning opportunities to ensure students feel respected and heard."

Yet, change is not fast and easy. It is important to keep in mind that moving away from traditional discipline and toward restorative discipline practices requires significant reforms in not only organizational practices, but also deep-seated beliefs. Principals seeking to implement a restorative justice program must remember to go slowly and be sure that community building is their foundation, as one cannot restore something one has not built. Before taking suspensions off the table, principals must be sure that they have something else to take their place. Too often, schools switch to a no-suspensions policy before building other systems to address misbehavior. This has led to chaos.

Leaders, teachers, students, and support staff must value the well-being of the school community as a top priority for the restorative justice approach to serve the community well. Collaborating and cooperating to build a strong and cohesive community is antithetical to mainstream American culture, which tends to focus on individual achievement and competition as opposed to teamwork and cooperation. Teaching the ways and means of such collective practices as restorative circles and mediation will take time, direct instruction, practice, community-building opportunities, and a reallocation of resources.

Although many municipalities are experimenting with restorative approaches, the entire U.S. justice system is based on determining guilt and allocating punishment. Americans are accustomed to that system. In handling justice differently in schools, educational leaders are creating a different system that may eventually inform the U.S. justice system, but society is not quite there yet. That point needs to be made clear to stakeholders.

Lastly, but perhaps most importantly, restorative practices have at their core a deep understanding of equity and social justice. As leaders embark on restorative justice training, it must be paired with social justice and cultural competence/humility training.

SHADOWING STUDENTS

One activity that can be effective and implemented quickly but is rarely used is to have secondary-school counselors shadow students. Although one primary role of a school counselor is to guide and advise students on their course selections, few have taken the time to visit and observe classes while in session. Many counselors have never set foot inside the chemistry lab or school gym during the class period. Furthermore, in most schools the counseling office is usually located in the administrative wing of the building, far from the classrooms. As a result, counselors remain isolated and distant from the classrooms. To break that isolation, introduce the idea of shadowing students to the pupil personnel and administrative staff, beginning with the school counselors.

Most counselors will be quick to see the merit in such an activity and generally be open to the idea, although some, of course, will argue that they do not have enough time to do so. Start by asking the counselors to select three of their counselees. The first student selected should have a rigorous schedule, be assigned to many honors or advanced-placement (AP) courses, be engaged in cocurricular activities and interscholastic programs, and have an excellent academic record. These are the students who are generally well liked by teachers and other students. Often, they are the student leaders.

The second student might be what is often referred to as an average student, one whose academic performance is satisfactory. A student who carries a modest number of challenging courses, and who engages in a limited number of cocurricular activities. The third student would be one with a history of struggling academically and socially, and who is suspected of having possible learning disabilities.

The intent of shadowing a student is for counselors to experience a day in the life of their counselees. The experience should result in the counselor gaining a greater appreciation of how the student navigates throughout the school day. They can witness the outcomes of their academic and social counseling now that they have had a firsthand experience of moving from class to class with their counselees. It is a powerful exercise that mirrors ethnographic research in that the counselors are able to immerse themselves in the day-to-day lives of their counselees.

In preparation for shadowing students, the principal must make it clear to the teachers and counselors that the purpose is to gain a firsthand understanding of what students experience in the course of a school day. The purpose is not for counselors to make judgments or evaluate teachers, but rather for the counselors to gain a better understanding and appreciation of the issues and challenges their counselees face during the school day.

Following the shadowing of their three students, counselors can share their observations with one another and, in doing so, improve their academic counseling skills. Students are most receptive to the idea, as are teachers, once they are assured of its purpose. For too long, classroom teachers have misunderstood the role and functions of the school counselor, in part because teacher–counselor interactions are often limited to when a crisis erupts between a teacher and student.

Principals will find that the exercise of shadowing students moves the counselors from their typical isolated location in the school. It increases their visibility and provides opportunities for them to interact with the classroom teachers. The experience allows the counselors and teachers to have a greater appreciation and understanding of one another's roles.

Likewise, principals, assistant principals, superintendents, and central office administrators would gain a much greater understanding and appreciation of student life in their schools if they too were to experience the process of shadowing a student. The more visible the school counselors and administrators are in classrooms, the more opportunities there are to interact with faculty and students to build a healthy and secure school culture.

THE OPEN HOUSE AND PARENT CONFERENCES

Research on family involvement in children's education has found that such involvement results in many positive benefits, including increased school attendance, higher academic performance, and improved attitudes toward school.[9] A long-standing practice by schools at every level is to reach out to parents by means of the parent–teacher conference and the annual open-house event. Neither is particularly powerful, but both are carried out as must-do rituals. Principals need to consider the limited return they receive for such efforts and, in turn, provide the leadership that will ensure that conferences and open-house events achieve their maximum potential.

Principals are sure to routinely schedule a day or an evening for parent–teacher conferences to take place. The event can serve as an effective outreach to parents and enhances a family's involvement in their child's education; however, conferences prove more effective when teachers are provided with some training on how best to confer with parents.

At the elementary level, parents are usually scheduled for a one-on-one meeting with their child's teacher. Rarely are teachers trained in how to conduct an effective parent–teacher conference beyond being handed a tip sheet on "dos and don'ts." The assumption is that teachers have no problems conducting conferences, given their formal teacher training. Moreover, the typical parent conference is generally scheduled in a manner that seriously restricts the time parents are allowed to meet with the teacher. It is not uncommon for parents to be scheduled for five- to 10-

minute conferences with their children's teachers at the elementary level, and the limited time frame available often prevents working parents from attending.

In secondary schools, where there is more than one teacher, parents often move through the evening following an abbreviated class schedule in which the periods are shortened to 10 to 12 minutes. It is just enough time for the teacher to briefly describe the curriculum requirements, their general expectations, and usually their grading rationale. It is clearly not intended for individual conferences to take place.

Depending on the teacher, parents report that the evening is boring, entertaining, or sometimes informative. Nevertheless, such open-house events rarely reveal how any specific child is performing in class. If parents wish to check on their children's progress, they can usually access the child's grades online or inundate the teacher with e-mails. The most effective approach is to schedule a conference with the teachers. The intention of the open house is to give parents some understanding of a typical day in school, as well as some familiarity with the physical school environment.

Principals and assistant principals should experience an open-house evening by following a student's schedule. One, either the principal or the assistant principal, should follow a parent whose child's schedule is rigorous, with many honors and AP classes. The other should follow a parent whose child is struggling or classified as learning disabled but is in the mainstream classes. They should be particularly aware of the parents' dispositions as they move through the students' schedules. The experience may result in ways to improve the open house for parents and faculty.

ADVISER/ADVISEE PROGRAMS

One way for middle and high schools to improve parent–teacher conferences is to implement a student adviser program in which personnel are assigned to advise a small group of 10 to 12 students. The adviser remains with the advisees from the time they enter school until the time they graduate. It is the adviser who then meets with the parents of their advisees and serves as the conduit to their advisees' teachers.

With a student adviser program in place, parents can be scheduled for longer conferences with the adviser. The expanded time is a result of each adviser having responsibility for a small group of students who they have come to know well. The typical secondary teacher may have 100 or more students who they meet every day. With their interactions more focused on instruction and covering the curriculum, it is difficult for teachers to get to know each student personally.

It is the advisers' responsibility to be fully aware of the academic progress of their advisees, as well as any possible social or emotional issues they are experiencing. They can, if necessary, schedule additional conferences with an advisee's subject-area teachers and parents. Although not very common, the student adviser program is a reform structure originally promoted by middle school educators.

There was little enthusiasm for the program from the start. Secondary principals reported that the teachers saw it as an additional job responsibility. In addition, the district feared they would be bogged down in prolonged negotiations with the teachers' bargaining unit, claiming it to be a change in working conditions. Although it was developed as a means to help middle school students adjust to a departmentalized structure, middle school principals have not been overly enthusiastic about promoting a teacher adviser program in their schools. The resistance to the program is even greater at the high school level, where teachers see the adviser role as being that of the school counselor; however, a student adviser program was never intended to replace the school counselors, but to lend needed support.

The lack of an adviser program is a great loss to students and their parents. It is a structure that high school principals should promote. An adviser program can improve the overall communications between the school and parents, and is well worth the costs, if any, to employ it in secondary schools. It is a far better way to ensure that parent–teacher conferences are focused and take place as needed. Lastly, one benefit of having an adviser/advisee program in place is that the adviser can relate positive information about a student to parents, in addition to concerns.

On the other hand, principals do encourage teachers to initiate a parent–teacher conference when a student is having a social or academic issue in class. Such a conference can be invaluable if conducted properly. Principals must be aware of these conferences and provide training to help teachers conduct effective parent–teacher meetings. Teachers need training and coaching, particularly in how to deliver "bad news" in a manner that minimizes parents' defensiveness and maximizes potential collaboration and problem-solving strategies.

Subjects covered in training should include active listening and strategies for defusing a confrontational parent. In some situations, it may be appropriate to conduct a three-way conference with the teacher, parent, and adviser. Furthermore, if appropriate, an administrator or school counselor can be requested to attend. Advisers and teachers should also be encouraged to compliment parents on how well they have supported and instilled the importance of schooling in their child. It is a good way to reinforce the educational values they are promoting in their homes.

Overall, principals recognize that single-day scheduled parent conferences have limited value for the parents who choose to attend and are often viewed by many teachers as a necessary irritant. Nevertheless, they remain intact in most schools and are carried out year after year. Nonetheless, if teachers are provided with training in how better to conduct individual parent–teacher conferences, the results can be gratifying for everyone involved and best serve the needs of students and parents.

LEADING SUCCESSFUL ORGANIZATIONAL CHANGE

Top-down and incremental changes have been cited in the literature as the primary reasons for the failure of leaders to bring about systemic change. If principals are to be successful change agents, they should establish a direction and vision that goes beyond increasing student achievement. They should develop a plan for long-term school development relying on shared leadership that builds their social capacity and mutual support to acquire new skills. By sharing knowledge and increasing interdependency among every segment of the school community, principals ensure that they have a greater chance to establish systemic change.[10]

The suggestions noted throughout this chapter and the book are presented in the spirit of helping today's principals navigate challenging times. The intent is never to lose the importance and value of their work as educators. After all, our most precious resource is our children. When children are educated in kind, caring, and compassionate school settings, they will remain lifelong learners and active good citizens capable of making their lives and those of the people in their communities safe, secure, and fruitful.

NOTES

1. Joseph A. Durlak et al., "The Impact of Enhancing Students' Social and Emotional Learning: A Meta-analysis of School-Based Universal Interventions," *Child Development* 82, no. 1 (February 2011): 405–32.

2. Matthew Dahlitz, "Prefrontal Cortex," *Neuropsychotherapist*, January 4, 2017, https://www.neuropsychotherapist.com/prefrontal-cortex/.

3. Juliette Berg, David Osher, Deborah Moroney, and Nick Yoder, *The Intersection of School Climate and Social and Emotional Development* (Washington: American Institutes for Research, 2017), https://www.air.org/sites/default/files/downloads/report/Intersection-School-Climate-and-Social-and-Emotional-Development-February-2017.pdf.

4. "General Mindfulness," *Department of Psychiatry Education, University of Massachusetts Medical School*, https://www.umassmed.edu/psychiatry/education/mindfulphysicianleadershipprogram/general-mindfulness/.

5. "Richie Davidson Is Stalking the Mediating Brain," *Mindful*, June 17, 2014, https://www.mindful.org/tracking-the-skill-of-well-being/.

6. Lisa Flook et al., "Mindfulness for Teachers: A Pilot Study to Assess Effects on Stress, Burnout, and Teaching Efficacy," *Mind, Brain, and Education* 7, no. 3 (September 2013): 10; Jill Ladwig, "Study Shows Mindfulness Training Can Help Reduce Teacher Stress and Burnout," *Center for Investigating Healthy Minds*, last modified August 28, 2013, https://news.wisc.edu/study-shows-mindfulness-training-can-help-reduce-teacher-stress-and-burnout/.

7. John Meiklejohn et al., "Integrating Mindfulness Training into K–12 Education: Fostering the Resilience of Teachers and Students," *Mindfulness* 3, no. 4 (2012): 291–307.

8. Patricia Leigh Brown, "Opening Up, Students Transform a Vicious Circle," *New York Times*, April 3, 2013, https://www.nytimes.com/2013/04/04/education/restorative-justice-programs-take-root-in-schools.html; Fania E. Davis, "Eight Tips for Schools Interested in Restorative Justice," *Edutopia*, September 26, 2014, https://www.edutopia.org/blog/restorative-justice-tips-for-schools-fania-davis.

9. Anne O'Brien, "The Importance of Community Involvement in Schools," *Edutopia*, March 21, 2012, https://www.edutopia.org/blog/community-parent-involvement-essential-anne-obrien; Reform Support Network, *Strategies for Community Engagement in School Turnaround* (Washington: U.S. Department of Education, 2014).

10. Michelle Jones and Alma Harris, "Principals Leading Successful Organizational Change," *Journal of Organizational Change Management* 27, no. 3 (May 2014): 473–85.

Appendix A
Principal's Questionnaire

PRINCIPAL'S QUESTIONNAIRE

The responses to the questionnaire are to be used as a tool for you and your colleagues to build a strong administrative team.

Urban __ Suburban __ Rural __

Student enrollment: _____

Number of staff you supervise: _____

1. What did you find to be the most challenging aspects of the job in your first year, and how did you overcome them?

_____

_____

2. What challenges have remained as you have become more experienced?

_____

_____

3. Did you receive sufficient coaching support from your superintendent or central office administrators as a new principal?

Superintendent Yes ___ No ___

Central office administrators Yes ___ No ___

4. Who do you go to if you have a serious personnel issue or concern?

Superintendent _____ Assistant superintendent _____ Colleagues _____ Assistant principal _____ Mentor _____ Other _____

5. Who do you rely on when a curriculum or instructional issue surfaces?

Superintendent _____ Assistant superintendent _____ Other principals _____ Assistant principal _____ Executive coach _____ District curriculum coordinator _____ Mentor _____ Colleagues _____

6. Rate *your* performance on the tasks below using the following four-point scale:

1) ineffective, 2) developing, 3) effective, 4) highly effective

Defining the school mission	1 __	2 __	3 __	4 __
Framing the school goals	1 __	2 __	3 __	4 __
Communicating the school goals	1 __	2 __	3 __	4 __
Annually assessing school goals	1 __	2 __	3 __	4 __
Coordinating the curriculum	1 __	2 __	3 __	4 __
Supervising and evaluating instruction	1 __	2 __	3 __	4 __
Monitoring student progress	1 __	2 __	3 __	4 __
Protecting instructional time	1 __	2 __	3 __	4 __
Providing recognition and praise for teachers	1 __	2 __	3 __	4 __
Providing rigorous academic programs	1 __	2 __	3 __	4 __
Providing for professional development	1 __	2 __	3 __	4 __
Maintaining a high level of visibility	1 __	2 __	3 __	4 __
Maintaining effective parent and community relations	1 __	2 __	3 __	4 __
Promoting social and emotional learning principles	1 __	2 __	3 __	4 __
Remaining current on educational theories and research	1 __	2 __	3 __	4 __

Maintaining a safe and secure school	1 __	2 __	3 __	4 __
Providing a clean and attractive school and grounds	1 __	2 __	3 __	4 __

7. What percentage of your time is consumed by the following four major job functions? The first column is labeled real time, and the second is the ideal time you would prefer. Be sure that each column totals 100% when completed.

REAL IDEAL

Administrative e.g., scheduling, budgeting, responding to e-mails, holding central office meetings, maintaining community interactions

%____ %____

Curriculum and Instructional Issues e.g., reviewing the curriculum, revising and implementing the program of studies, providing instructional resources and professional programs on effective instructional practices

%____ %____

Supervising, Coaching, and Evaluating Personnel e.g., visiting classrooms, writing written observations, making formal and informal contacts with teachers and students

%____ %____

Pupil Personnel Issues e.g., addressing disruptive student behaviors, managing special education placement and services, holding parent conferences

%____ %____

Total..%100 %100

8. How do you remain current on sound education practices and research?

Active membership in state and national organizations ___ Attendance at conferences and workshops ___ Reading the literature ___ Other ___

9. Does your *superintendent* encourage you to belong to professional organizations and support your attendance at conferences and workshops?

Never ___ Sometimes ___ Insist on appropriate memberships and attendance at conferences and workshops___

If so, which do you subscribe to, and which ones do you find most helpful?

10. Do you encourage your faculty and staff to belong to professional organizations and attend conferences and workshops?

No ___ Sometimes ___ Insist on appropriate memberships and attendance at conferences and workshops

11. In general, which of the three types of power do *you* and your *superintendent* rely on most when faced with a problem or challenge? Rank them in terms of use:

1) never used; 2) sometimes used; 3) most often used

	Superintendent	Principal
Positional power (the power of the office)	_____	_____
Personal power (one's persona and emotional intelligence)	_____	_____
Knowledge (resourcefulness, expertise, and experience)	_____	_____

How do you think teachers would describe your use of power when faced with a problem or challenge?

Positional ___ Personal ___ Knowledge ___

12. Do *you* or your *superintendent* subscribe to a particular theory of educational leadership?

Yes ___ No ___

13. Which description best fits *you* and your *superintendent's* leadership style?

	Principal	Superintendent
Highly directive and highly supportive	_____	_____
Rarely directive and highly supportive	_____	_____
Highly directive and rarely supportive	_____	_____

Rarely directive and rarely supportive   ____   ____

14. Do you have anything to add regarding your experiences as a school principal?

_____

_____

Appendix B
Superintendent's Questionnaire

PRINCIPAL'S QUESTIONNAIRE

Urban __ Suburban __ Rural __
Total student population: _____

1. What did you find to be the most challenging aspects of the job in your first year?

_____

_____

2. What challenges have remained as you have become more experienced?

_____

_____

3. How did you overcome these challenges?

_____

_____

4. Which of the following best prepared you for the superintendency:

Graduate school ___ Prior administrative experience ___
Mentoring support ___

5. Who do you generally go to in the district if you have a serious personnel issue or concern?

School attorney ___ Board chair ___ Assistant superintendent ___

6. Who do you generally rely on when a curriculum or instructional issue surfaces?

Assistant superintendent ___ Principals ___ Other superintendents ___
Teachers ___

7. Rate *your* performance on the tasks below using the following four-point scale:

1) ineffective; 2) developing; 3) effective; 4) highly effective

Task	1	2	3	4
Defining the district mission	1__	2__	3__	4__
Framing the district goals	1__	2__	3__	4__
Annually assessing district goals	1__	2__	3__	4__
Communicating the district goals	1__	2__	3__	4__
Managing the instructional program	1__	2__	3__	4__
Coordinating the curriculum	1__	2__	3__	4__
Supervising and evaluating instruction	1__	2__	3__	4__
Monitoring student progress	1__	2__	3__	4__
Developing a district learning climate	1__	2__	3__	4__
Protecting instructional time	1__	2__	3__	4__
Providing recognition and praise for administrators	1__	2__	3__	4__
Promoting rigorous academic programs	1__	2__	3__	4__
Providing for professional development	1__	2__	3__	4__
Maintaining high visibility	1__	2__	3__	4__
Overseeing the instructional programs	1__	2__	3__	4__

Supervising and evaluating personnel	1 __	2 __	3 __	4 __
Monitoring student progress	1 __	2 __	3 __	4 __
Being an Effective Change Agent	1 __	2 __	3 __	4 __
Being an effective decision maker	1 __	2 __	3 __	4 __
Providing professional development for faculty and staff	1 __	2 __	3 __	4 __
Maintaining effective community relations	1 __	2 __	3 __	4 __
Maintaining safe and secure schools	1 __	2 __	3 __	4 __
Maintaining clean and attractive buildings and grounds	1 __	2 __	3 __	4 __

8. In general, what percentage of your time is consumed by the following responsibilities?

Interacting and Meeting with the Board of Education e.g., regularly scheduled public meetings, executive sessions, subcommittee meetings, phone calls, written correspondence

% ____

Administrative Functions e.g., constructing board agendas, addressing policy issues and concerns, scheduling, budgeting, interviewing candidates, handling personal issues and grievances, negotiating contracts, attending staff meetings, attending school and public events

% ____

Curriculum and Instructional Issues e.g., meeting to discuss curriculum issues and concerns, ensuring implementation of program of studies, providing instructional resources, providing professional programs regarding effective instruction

% ____

Supervising, Coaching, and Evaluating Personnel e.g., visiting schools, writing written evaluations, making formal and informal contacts with administrators, faculty, and staff

% ____

District Issues e.g., addressing special education, capital projects, maintenance of buildings and grounds, and changing demographics

% ____

Community Outreach e.g., advisory committees, parent associations, booster clubs, civic groups

% ____

Total % 100

9. Have you ever spent time shadowing a secondary student for the day?

Yes __ No __

10. Do you schedule regular school visits?

Yes __ No __

11. When you visit schools, do you visit classrooms as well?

Yes __ No __

12. In general, which of the three types of power do you rely on most when faced with a problem or challenge? Rank them in terms of use:

1) never used; 2) sometimes used; 3) most often used

Positional power (the power of the office) _____

Personal power (your persona and emotional intelligence) _____

Knowledge (resourcefulness, access and storage of information, expertise) _____

13. How do you think the principals would describe your use of power?

Positional ___ Personal ___ Knowledge ___

14. Do you subscribe to a particular theory of educational leadership?

Yes __ No __

15. Which description best fits your leadership style?

Highly directive and highly supportive	___	___
Rarely directive and highly supportive	___	___
Highly directive and rarely supportive	___	___
Rarely directive and rarely supportive	___	___

16. What professional organizations do you subscribe to, and which ones do you find most influence your work?

_____

17. How do you remain current on educational practices and research?

        Participation in state and national organizations ___
              Reading the literature ___ Other ___

18. Which, if any, organization has been most helpful to you?

_____

19. Do you require the principals to be active participants in their professional organizations?

                                                    Yes ___ No ___

20. Do you have anything you wish to add regarding your experiences with school principals?

_____

_____

_____

Appendix C
Teacher's Questionnaire

TEACHER'S QUESTIONNAIRE

Provide the information requested and answer the questions regarding your experiences in your most recent place of employment, as well as your opinions and observations of your principal, who may or may not be your immediate supervisor.

Employment status:
    Currently employed ___ Retired ___ Resigned ___
If you resigned, please explain why:

_____

_____

Experience: Position: _____
    Number of years: ____
    Area of the country: Northeast___ South___ Midwest___ West___
        Urban_____ Suburban _____ Rural _____
                          Grade or Subject: _____
    Student/teacher ratio: 1:15____ 1:20 ____ 1:25 ____ 1:30 ____ 1:35+ ____

1. What did you find to be the most challenging aspects of teaching?

_____

Teacher's Questionnaire

2. What challenges have remained as you have become a more experienced teacher?

_____

_____

3. Which of the following people did you find most resourceful in helping you to overcome these challenges?

Colleagues___ Department chair ___ Assistant principal ___ Principal ___ Professional organizations ___ School-assigned coach ___ Graduate instructor ___

4. How much coaching and support did you receive from your immediate supervisor or principal as a new teacher?

None ___ Very little ___ Adequate ___ Excellent and effective ___

5. Who do you go to if you have a serious problem with a student?

Principal ___ Teaching colleague ___ School counselor or psychologist ___ Assistant principal ___ Department chair ___ Other ___

6. Who do you rely on when a curriculum or instructional issue surfaces?

Principal ___ Colleagues ___ Department chair ___ Professional literature ___ School-assigned coach ___ Other ___

7. Rate your *principal's* performance on the tasks below using the following scale:

1) ineffective; 2) developing; 3) effective; 4) highly effective; don't know (DK)

Defining the school mission	1 ___	2 ___	3 ___	4 ___	DK ___
Framing the school goals	1 ___	2 ___	3 ___	4 ___	DK ___
Communicating the school goals	1 ___	2 ___	3 ___	4 ___	DK ___
Annually assessing school goals	1 ___	2 ___	3 ___	4 ___	DK ___

Coordinating the curriculum	1 __	2 __	3 __	4 __	DK __
Supervising and evaluating instruction	1 __	2 __	3 __	4 __	DK __
Monitoring student progress	1 __	2 __	3 __	4 __	DK __
Protecting instructional time	1 __	2 __	3 __	4 __	DK __
Providing recognition and praise for teachers	1 __	2 __	3 __	4 __	DK __
Providing rigorous academic programs	1 __	2 __	3 __	4 __	DK __
Providing for professional development	1 __	2 __	3 __	4 __	DK __
Maintaining a high level of visibility	1 __	2 __	3 __	4 __	DK __
Maintaining effective parent relations	1 __	2 __	3 __	4 __	DK __
Promoting social and emotional learning	1 __	2 __	3 __	4 __	DK __
Remaining current on educational research	1 __	2 __	3 __	4 __	DK __
Maintaining a safe and secure school	1 __	2 __	3 __	4 __	DK __
Providing clean and attractive school facilities	1 __	2 __	3 __	4 __	DK __

8. What percentage of your principal's time would you estimate is consumed by the following major job functions?

DK __ Can make following estimates:_____

Administrative Functions e.g., scheduling, budgeting, responding to e-mails

% ____

Curriculum and Instructional Issues e.g., reviewing the curriculum, revising and implementing the program of studies, providing instructional resources and professional programs on effective instructional practices

% ____

Supervising, Coaching, and Evaluating Personnel e.g., visiting classrooms, making observations, making formal and informal contacts with teachers and students

% ____

Pupil Personnel Issues e.g., addressing disruptive student behaviors, special education placement and parent conferences

% ____
Total %100

9. Does your principal encourage teachers to hold memberships in professional organizations and attend conferences and workshops?

Never __ Sometimes __
Insists on appropriate professional memberships__
Encourages attendance at national, state, and local conferences and workshops
Never __ Sometimes __ Always __

10. Which, if any, of the professional organizations have been most helpful to you?

_____

_____

11. In general, which of the three types of power does your principal rely on most when faced with a problem or challenge? Rank them in terms of use:

1) never used; 2) sometimes used; 3) most often used

Positional power (authority and controls) ____
Personal power (one's persona and emotional intelligence) ____
Knowledge (resourcefulness and expertise) ____

12. Which of the three types of power would students cite as most exercised by the principal?

Positional ___ Personal ___ Knowledge ___

13. Does your principal subscribe to and express a particular approach or theory of leadership, for example, servant leadership, ethical leadership, distributive leadership, or transformational leadership?

Yes ___ No___ Don't know ___ If yes, please indicate the leadership theory practiced.

_____

14. Which description best fits the leadership style of your principal?

Highly directive and highly supportive	____	____
Rarely directive and highly supportive	____	____
Highly directive and rarely supportive	____	____
Rarely directive and rarely supportive	____	____

15. Do you have anything you wish to add regarding your experiences and interactions with your school principal?

_____

_____

Appendix D
Principal's Survey

PRINCIPAL'S SURVEY

Urban ____ Suburban ____ Rural ___

Enrollment in Your School: _____

1. Would you complete the questionnaire and participate in the process by sharing your responses with your superintendent and teachers?

1) Yes ___ 2) No ___ 3) Under certain conditions ___ If 3, please explain

_____

_____

2. Did you find the questionnaire to fairly reflect the work and challenges principals encounter?

1) Yes ___ 2) No ___ 3) Somewhat ___ If 3, what would you add or delete?

_____

_____

3. Do you have a similar process in place in your district?

1) Yes ___ 2) No ___ 3) Somewhat similar ___ If 3, please describe

_____

_____

4. Would the superintendent in your district subscribe to this process by completing his/her questionnaire and sharing it with you?

   1) Yes ___ 2) No ___ 3) With modifications ___ If 3 what would they be?

   _____

   _____

5. Would your teachers subscribe to this process?

   1) Yes ___ 2) No ___

6. Do you have leadership teams in your school? A leadership team is a school-based group of teachers and the principal who work to provide a strong organizational process for school renewal and improvement.

   1) Yes ___ 2) No ___

   Please add any comments or suggestions.

   _____

   _____

   _____

   _____

Appendix E
Classroom Climate Survey: Grades 4–12

CLASSROOM CLIMATE SURVEY: GRADES 4–12

Teacher's name (required): _____
Student's name (optional): _____

As your teacher, I want to know how you feel about what goes on in our class. Using the information you give me, I can make improvements. Thank you!

1. Do you like coming to class?

Yes ___ Most of the time ___ Not really ___ No ___ If you said no, please explain why.

_____

_____

2. Do you feel safe in class?

All of the time ___ Most of the time ___ Sometimes ___ Never ___ If you said never, please explain why.

_____

_____

3. Do you feel the classroom rules are fair?

   Yes ___ No ___ What rules do you think are not fair?

   _____

   _____

4. Is the class quiet enough for you to do your work?

   All of the time ___ Most of the time ___ Sometimes ___ Never ___ If you said never, please explain why.

   _____

   _____

5. Are your neighbors considerate of your personal space?

   All of the time ___ Most of the time ___ Sometimes ___ Never ___

6. Does the teacher call on you enough when you raise your hand?

   All of the time ___ Most of the time ___ Sometimes ___ Never ___

7. Do you feel comfortable talking to your teacher?

   All of the time ___ Most of the time ___ Sometimes ___ Never ___ If you said never, please explain.

   _____

   _____

8. How do you feel about the subjects you learn in class?

   Enjoy and find very interesting ___ All right ___ Hard to understand ___ Boring ___

9. Do you feel that you have friends in class?

   Many ___ A few ___ None ___

10. How often do you work in groups?

   Every day ___ Most days ___ Rarely ___ Never ___

11. How often are you assigned homework?

   Every day ___ Most days ___ Rarely ___ Never ___

12. Is the homework helpful and interesting?

   Always ___ Most of the time ___ Sometimes ___ Never ___

13. What would you change about your class if you could?

_____

_____

Appendix F

West Windsor/Plainsboro Regional School District, New Jersey, High School Bell Schedule

Entrance bell	7:35	
Class 1	7:40–8:40	60 minutes
Class 2	8:45–9:45	60 minutes
Class 3	9:50–10:50	60 minutes
Lunch	10:54–11:35	41 minutes
Class 4	11:40–12:40	60 minutes
Class 5	12:45–1:45	60 minutes
Class 6	1:50–2:50	60 minutes

Appendix G
No Substitute Policy and Six Class Meetings per Day

With the exception of a long-term teacher absence, students of an absent teacher report to a common area supervised by two proctors. Students are expected to use the time to follow up on assigned work given by the absent teacher to complete in place of having a substitute in their class.

The eight-period schedule operates with only six classes meeting for one hour a day. The hour class time allows for deeper learning to take place and labs to be an hour and 20 minutes, with AP labs lasting two hours. All students have a study hall to offer music lessons, guidance groups, and study skills for students with learning differences

A Day	B Day	C Day	D Day		
4	3	2	1	7:40–8:40	Hr. 1
1	4	3	2	8:45–9:45	Hr. 2
2	1	4	3	9:50–10:50	Hr. 3
LUNCH		10:55–11:35			
8	7	6	5	11:40–12:40	Hr. 4
5	8	7	6	12:45–1:45	Hr. 5
6	8	7		1:50–2:50	Hr. 6

When a science lab backs up to lunch, the third-hour or fourth-hour class is extended 20 minutes.

Dennis J. Lepold
Principal
West Windsor – Plainsboro HS South

About the Author

John T. Fitzsimons, with fifty years of experience as a pubic educator, has served as a teacher, principal, and school superintendent, in Connecticut, New Jersey, and New York. He holds a Ph.D. in Language and Literacy from Fordham University and has recently served on the New York City District 3 Community Board of Education as an appointee of the Manhattan Borough President.

www.ingramcontent.com/pod-product-compliance
Lightning Source LLC
Chambersburg PA
CBHW030144240426
43672CB00005B/261